FISHING DOGS

·

A GUIDE TO THE
HISTORY, TALENTS, AND TRAINING
OF THE BAILDALE, THE FLOUNDERHOUNDER,
THE ANGLER DOG, AND SUNDRY OTHER
BREEDS OF AQUATIC DOGS
(*CANIS PISCATORIUS*)

·

Raymond Coppinger

illustrated by Peter Pinardi

1🍥
Ten Speed Press
Berkeley, California

Ten Speed Press
P.O. Box 7123
Berkeley, CA 94707

Distributed in Canada by Publishers Group West

Cover design by Toni Tajima

Text design by Victor Ichioka

Printed in the United States

Library of Congress Cataloging in Publication Data

Coppinger, Raymond
Fishing dogs / by Raymond Coppinger ; illustrated by Peter Pinardi
    p.   cm.
ISBN 0-89815-842-7
1. Dogs. 2. Dogs—Humor. 3. Fishing stories. I. Pinardi, Peter. II. Title
SF426.2.C67 1996
799.1'0207—dc20   96-13934
                              CIP

1 2 3 4 5 — 99 98 97 96

· CONTENTS ·

Dedication and Acknowledgments

•

Since I can't think of any one better,
I dedicate this book to Stan Warner.

•

Will Ryan (FSW) has been pretty dedicated to this book, too, and took out most of the references to sex and hunters.

When I first sent the book to the publisher, I put the paragraphs in a different order as kind of a test. Clancy Drake, the editor, saw right through the scheme and put them back the original way. So any mistakes you find in this book are probably hers.

Many books have the author's name on the cover, and underneath it says, "As told to...." This one should be, "As told to, and retold to, and reretold to Lorna Coppinger." I had to in order for her to get it right.

· FOREWORD ·

Several years ago, I decided I should try fishing. It seemed like reasonably cheap therapy. There was this guy at the office, Stan, who is a fisherman, and I asked him if he'd teach me how to fish. He said yes.

Stan taught me some of the basics, like, when you're in a boat in the middle of the pond you cast toward the shore, and when you're on the shore you cast toward the middle of the pond. It all made sense, and I quickly became a great fisherman, often bringing home little trophies that convinced my wife I was a good forager. Stan and I began to search for trophies together and it wasn't long before we became fishing buddies.

"Fishing buddies" is an important concept. If you do catch and release fishing, it is important to have someone trustworthy around to verify that you actually did release something. Trustworthiness is the foundation of male-to-male bonding. At its best, male-to-male bonding means that if your buddy sets his hook in your butt he won't run off or pass out, but will remove the hook with a certain seriousness. It's okay to joke about it later when you tell all your friends what a good time you had, but the actual hook extraction scene happens with the silent formality of two men who know exactly what to do and what not to say.

There are two axioms in the institution of fishing buddies. The first is, good fishing buddies are hard to find. I once asked Stan if he'd ever had a fishing buddy before me, and he admitted that he'd fooled around a little bit, but never anything serious. I was kind of touched by this at the time, until I figured out the second axiom for myself: no fishing buddy is perfect, including Stan.

Stan's biggest problem is breakfast: he's committed to it, and it is always too big, too messy, and too late. His other big problem is knowing where to put something in the van. He packs objects according to when we will use them. The van-packing process should be like looking at life backwards: the first thing you want to use should be the last thing you pack. But Stan has the habit of packing first what we'll need right away. For example, he always wants to have breakfast before going fishing, and the breakfast stuff is under the fishing stuff, which is under the rainy day stuff on clear days and right by the sun block on rainy days. It's just not the way I like to run my life, that's all.

Once we tried a trial separation. Stan went off to this faraway lake at five A.M. and sat in the local diner until these two old guys, seeing he was buddyless, took pity on him and asked if he wanted to join them for the day. After several hours on the lake, according to Stan, one guy apologized for the other, who was not much of a fisherman and had in fact drifted off to sleep in the middle of a long cast. The guy told Stan that he was breaking in a new buddy because his old one had died, and he figured at his age he couldn't be all that fussy. It set Stan to thinking of that old expression, "After forty your chances of getting fulminated in an aluminum canoe are better than your chances of finding a good fishing buddy."

There was a lesson in that for both of us. During our trial separation, our wives suggested some professional counseling. One thing led to another, and our therapist suggested that maybe we should adopt a kid to take fishing with us. That seemed a little extreme to me, mainly because of the size of the boat, but when I suggested that we adopt a Swedish cook who actually *liked* peeling welded potatoes off the pan, or that we should limit our fishing to ponds behind all-night diners, everybody got mad at me.

Finally she (the therapist) suggested a dog. She wasn't all that experienced in counseling fishing buddies, but she'd had some success with childless couples and pets, and she thought it might work for us. I thought a dog might be a good solution: maybe a dog could at least get the burned home fries off the bottom of the pan. So I said I'd be willing to give it a try.

That is how we decided to get a fishing dog: a dog that would not only help us get our minds off of one another's faults (like Stan's looking for weeds and lily pads in the spring, just to mention one of his little hang-ups), but also help us with our fishing.

Stan, being the economist, said he'd pay for half the dog if I, the biologist, could find the right one. Since I was really into making this relationship work, I did some diligent research on fishing dogs. When I started my research, I didn't know if real fishing dogs even existed. Oh, I knew the dog paddle, but I mean breeds of dogs that do specialized tasks.

Being a scholar, I went first to the technical journals to see what other cultures had done in the way of breeding dogs to help with fishing. But because anthropologists study hunters and gatherers and not fishers and gatherers, there is no history of fishing dogs.

I quickly became amazed at how much has been written on hunting dogs, while almost nothing has been written on fishing dogs. Almost everything about these dogs is word of mouth. Eventually I talked to dozens of breeders and sportsmen about their fishing dogs and I was forced to come to this conclusion: you don't hear about fishing dogs because all the fishing dog breeds have been successful, therefore there's no need to register them with the American Kennel Club, and also no reason to write a lot of articles in the sporting magazines trying to prove how great they are.

Some of my first leads on tracking down the story of fishing dogs were literary, not scientific. For instance, Lord Home[1] tells the story of an early relative of his (probably the guy they named the house after, even though we all know a

---

1 Home, Alec Douglas-Home, Baron. *Border Reflections, Chiefly on the Arts of Shooting and Fishing.* Illustrated by Roger McPhail. London: Collins, 1979.

Home is not a house). The earl was noted for landing a sixty-nine-and-a-half-pound salmon with his twenty-two-foot salmon rod and horsehair line (fly fishermen can probably back-order it from Orvis; I like Appaloosa myself). Lord Home the earlier

> *…owned a dog which became notorious and then famous. It would sit on the river bank at the mill stream opposite Wark castle, and in a morning's fishing it would catch and land twenty or more salmon and lay them at its owner's feet. The jealous, humorless and irate owner of the South Bank of the river brought a law-suit against the dog; the case being known as 'Lord Tankerville versus a dog—the property of the Earl of Home'. Much to the joy of the Scottish side the dog won.*

Lord Home the later (but now, the late) had a retriever "…which landed salmon by gripping them across the gills and delivering them to hand." If the Brits hadn't already invented all the dogs they were going to (see page 3), this dog could have been the founding sire of a breed of salmon retrievers, which would have made fishermen's lives more enjoyable and safer. Dogs that retrieve fish would reduce the necessity of carrying nets, which make the bottom of many a boat a veritable foot-snare. A field trial champion–equivalent salmon retriever would do all the fishing, and the owner wouldn't even need to go near the water, which is safer yet.

Think about it for a minute. Suppose there comes a day when you would like to go fishing, but for one reason or another you have to stay home and mow the lawn. If you had a trained descendent of Lord Home's retriever, you could send him out by himself. Imagine the thrill of waiting at the door on a Saturday night, anxious to see just what luck he had.

Now suppose your fishing buddy couldn't go that day, either (windows). Then his dog could go with yours. You would have to make sure both dogs obeyed creel limits, so they would have to be able to tell the difference between a smallmouth and a largemouth bass. (Of course if your dogs were into catch and release, there would be no creel problem.)

If Home's hounds had become a reality, fishermen could be judged by the quality of their dogs, just like other sportsmen. Hunters have the wintertime pleasure of seeing their gun and their deer head mounted in mute splendor over the mantelpiece, while their retriever lies curled up by the fire with its feet twitching. The best a catch and release fisherman can do is call his fishing buddy, who'd probably rather watch the Celtics game than hear again how I caught last summer's first fish, last fish, biggest fish, and smallest fish.

In any case, Lord Home's story was an inspiration to me in my research. If there was one dog that could retrieve and deliver salmon to hand, then there must be others that could help out with other fishing chores. Now, years later,

Stan and I are still fishing together, and we are also experts on fishing dogs.

I've written a lot about working dogs, but even as I have become more and more famous as a fisherman, nobody has ever asked me to write about the fishing dogs. I met Ed Zern at an award ceremony once, and even though he could have asked me, he didn't. He never even mentioned the fact that I hadn't written about fishing dogs. My friend Will Ryan, another famous sports writer (FSW), who would write about carp if he had to, has always remained mute on the subject.

It's like the dog paddle: practically everybody knows the dog paddle. The dog paddle is the most famous helper of fishermen, and it is often the first piece of boating equipment that young sportsmen gain proficiency with. It is so common that people out on the lake in an emergency will go instinctively for the dog paddle. When I go anywhere near the water I always have mine with me. Not only does the dog paddle propel you through the water, but it is self-portaging around rapids, a truly amazing combination. But, as far as I know, nobody has actually written: "The dog paddle is a self-propelling, fully independent locomotory system and everybody who goes near the water should have one and know how to use it."

As I'll demonstrate in this book, specialized breeds of fishing dogs, unlike the dog paddle, don't just happen. The evolution of each was slow, following a logical progression from an ancient form into the modern, highly specialized form. Since the early forms weren't any good, fishermen didn't notice them and therefore made no mention of them. But as centuries passed and the breeds evolved, getting better and better at their tasks, fishermen began to sit up and think about how to use and improve them.

This isn't surprising. The same kind of revelation happens with hunting dogs. How many times have you been sitting by the fire reading a book, when a pack of coonhounds goes by under the window. "What's that?" you say. "Dogs," says the wife. "Must be chasing a raccoon," you muse; "I didn't know we had coonhounds." "I guess we do now," she says. That's the way it is with evolution. You get up one morning, completely unsuspecting, and find somebody has discovered a new dog. And once you start looking for them, fishing dog breeds start bobbing up all over. This book is the first attempt to put these discoveries in phylogenetic order.

There are some things people tend to lie about: their children, their cars, their dogs. Everybody's child is above average, everybody's car gets better gas mileage than mine, and everybody's dog is more intelligent than their kid. Well, fishing dogs really are worlds better than hunting dogs. I've searched the globe for the best and I don't think I'm stretching the truth on this.

You can dismiss this book as hypothetical if you want, but believe me, it is not. I wrote this book for the expert— the serious biologist and anthropologist—as well as for other fishermen interested in the bio-cultural evolution of man's best friend. If parts of it seem farfetched to you, well, that's science.

Also, as Stan always says, "You can't please every-body"—and he should know.

DOG PADDLE (SELF-PORTAGING)

FISHING DOG FAMILY TREE

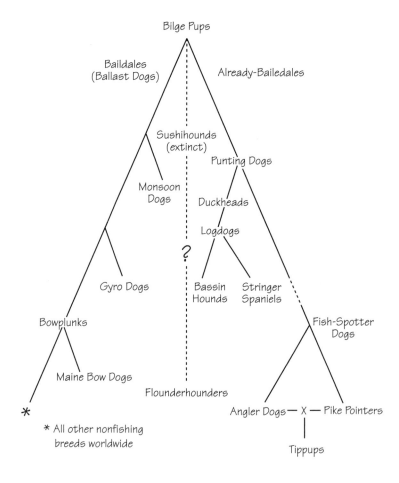

Introduction to the Fishing Dogs

BECAUSE I'M A DOG BIOLOGIST, I HAVE TO START BY EX-plaining how we got dogs in the first place. Most anthropologists now agree that dogs were the first domesticated animals.[1] Some anthropologists believe that the dog was the first step in the invention of civilization. This is because early training for domestication of dogs required the oak hoe handle and the two-by-four. These two tools also inspired dog trainers to cultivate soil and build houses. Some other anthropologists think houses had to come first, because you needed somewhere to take the wolf pups once you removed them from the den. The pups also needed to have a backyard where they could practice barking in order to become dogs. Whichever version you believe, it should be clear that evolution has favored dogs and barking, while two-by-fours and backyards have become noticeably smaller.

---

1 When it is said that most anthropologists agree, this does not mean they agree with each other. It simply means a preferential vote was taken on the question and dogs received the highest ranking even though nobody actually ranked them first. A couple of anthropologists actually tried using data, but it is difficult to use data and be democratic at the same time.

Hunter-foragers have spent a lot of time developing their dogs. In fact, scientists now claim that hunters took the first wolf pups out of their dens over 12,000 years ago and made them into hunting dogs. My field guide to the dogs lists 324 breeds of dog, and almost three quarters of them (240, to be exact) are hunting breeds. That means hunters have developed one new breed of hunting dog on average every fifty years since that first Mesolithic hunter acquired his first wolf pup. (Part of the reason hunters have created so many breeds is that they knew if they failed they could simply turn the breed over the to AKC for incorporation in the show and pet classes.)

It's sometimes hard to believe that the different breeds of dogs have taken on their shapes and colors because people wanted them to. Take, for example, the basset hound. You would think that some kind of genetic accident led to this deformation of the wolf, or that the ancestral basset committed a sin in a previous life and God punished him and his progeny for eternity. But prehistoric people wanted the basset hound to have short legs, so they bred short-legged animals to shorter-legged animals and just kept doing it until they finally got an animal that not only looked like a basset hound but acted like a basset hound. Various cultures eventually came up with different ways of breeding dogs, some of which are discussed below.

THE BRITISH SYSTEM OF DOMESTICATING DOGS

Since the Victorian age, the British system of domesticating dogs has been based on the *principle of natural selection*, which was invented in the nineteenth century by Alfred Wallace (1823–1913) in England (although Charles Darwin (1809–1882), another Englishman, managed to get more publicity than Wallace for coming up with the same idea at the same time). When the principle of natural selection is applied to domestic animals, especially dogs, it should be called **unnatural selection**. This is certainly obvious in the cases of the basset hound and the shar-pei.

The Wallaceo-Darwinian system of breeding dogs by natural selection is well over a hundred years old now and is holding up pretty well in England, though it is such a slow process that since it was invented the English have developed very few breeds of dogs; among them are some terriers and, of course, the old English sheepdog. The Brits have a name for gradual processes: "tradition." They also know how long tradition lasts, so they called this new breed "Olde Englishe Sheepdogge" right from the start.

THE FRENCH SYSTEM OF DOMESTICATING DOGS

The basset hound is not British; it's French. In France they have a very effective system of evolution working for them, and they have developed many different breeds. (Some say that the French have almost as many breeds of dogs as they have dogs.) The French System was the brainchild of Jean Baptiste Pierre Antoine de Monet chevalier de Lamarck (1744-1829). It is called the *theory of inheritance of acquired characteristics.*

Lamarck believed that an organism passes on to its offspring those characteristics which help it survive in its environment. On their way to becoming bassets, wolves could pass on their short-leggedness to their offspring by setting a good example while they were alive. In other words, if wolves worked hard to get ahead, and acquired short legs, then they could leave those legs to their kids. Thus, one didn't have to wait around a long time for basset hounds, as one does now.

Lamarck theorized that wolves were sick of living in the wild (especially as there wasn't much wild left in France). He stated that, in fact, wolves really wanted to be dogs. And as most of us learned from our mothers, you can be anything you want to if you want it enough. Wolves simply had to start behaving the way they wanted to look and they soon started to look the way they were behaving, thus evolving into the 324 (so far) breeds of dog. The process still works today.

As many of you know, dogs have a great desire to please their masters, and the masters reward this desire. Thus, if a dog is behaving like a beagle, but looks like a red setter, then the owner is displeased with the dog because he thinks that a dog that looks like a red setter should be acting like a red setter. Since it is acting like a beagle, then it is misbehaving and needs to be disciplined. Of course, even if it were acting like a red setter, it might still be disciplined, because no dog should want to please its master by acting like a red setter.

It is impossible to know which breed of hunting dog early man trained the first domesticated wolf cubs to be. That means the wolf pups didn't know at first what they were supposed to look like. The problem was further complicated by the fact that early man didn't know at first what dogs were supposed to look like, either—nor did early man know a lot about hunting (which has remained true to the present time). That means they didn't know what the different breeds were going to turn out to be, so they didn't know if the wolf puppies were behaving properly or not. Since the wolf cubs were going to turn into 240 different breeds of hunting dogs alone, then it must have been really confusing for the domesticators to know which one they were working on at any given time. No doubt this is why so many bird dogs chase deer.

In scientific terms, chasing deer is a displacement activity. A displacement activity is something you do to look busy when you don't really know what you should be doing— and if you don't know what you are doing, how on earth would you know what to look like? So the general rule for hunting dogs is: if you don't know what you're doing, displace a deer.

THE GERMAN SYSTEM OF DOMESTICATING DOGS

The Germans have their own system of breeding dogs and are the only people actively producing new breeds of dogs. While the English are still trying to perfect their last legitimate breed and by their own admission have a long way to go, and the French are still trying to find names for the breeds they have already invented, the Germans methodically create registered, brand-name dogs at a regular rate. The German shepherd and the Doberman pinscher are just two of their recent creations.

The Germans invent new dogs by averaging old breeds. They take two different purebreeds and cross them, producing a new mean ($\times$). Crossed dogs don't always produce a new mean breed immediately, so the breeders cross the crosses and get a thoroughly mean breed. The standard deviations are difficult to calculate, but surely the rottweiler is one.

Since Germans are concerned with breed purity, they breed only purebred dogs to other purebred dogs in order to get a new purebred: a dog representing the average, or mean, of the parents. Take the Doberman pinscher, for example. Herr (Mr.) Ludwig Dobermann was a tax collector in the 1860s. In order to protect himself, he created a truly mean dog by breeding purebred Great Danes with purebred German shepherds,[2] plus a little purebred rottweiler, some purebred beauceron,[3] and a touch of purebred English greyhound.[4]

There is more to the story, which the Germans freely admit, but they forgot to write it down. They also forgot the recipe for how much of each breed needs to be included, so it is now impossible to recreate a mean Doberman and we have to stick with the one we have. Only by breeding Dobermans to Dobermans can we preserve the original proportions and have conservation of the mean, which is important in keeping Dobermans up to standard.

THE ITALIAN SYSTEM OF DOMESTICATING DOGS

The Italian system is one of the quickest and most practical systems of dog development in the world: you don't actually do any breeding at all. Simply take any dog and name it after a vegetable. Follow the dog around until it finds the vegetable, and pesto, you've got a breed. The most famous example is

---

2 The purebred German shepherd itself was originally created by breeding together all the purebred sheep herding and sheep guarding dogs west of the Urals and then allowing them to mate spontaneously with purebred wolves.

3 A French wolf that wanted to be a sheepdog—lots of wolves want to be sheepdogs because it is easier to get close to sheep if you're a sheepdog.

4 Greyhounds from England were borrowed from the Egyptians long before the English learned about unnatural selection.

the truffle hound. A few years ago people in Italy were following little mongrel dogs around as the dogs looked for the mushrooms they were named after. Just recently, these dogs became a breed. That was quick! But the bad news is that the Italians are trying to register them with the IKC, so I guess the dogs didn't find many truffles after all.

The Italians have developed several breeds this way. There is the Roman molasses dog, which is now registered. The spumoni Italiano hound looks like ice cream even though it hasn't found any yet, and then of course there is the broccolio Italiano.

THE NORTH AMERICAN SYSTEM OF DOMESTICATING DOGS[5]

Americans think of dog evolution very simply. In the beginning God created heaven and earth. Then he made Adam and Eve. Then he made all the breeds of dogs. Then God created the oak hoe handle and the two-by-four so Man would have dominion over the dog. And God knows they needed it.

Realizing that God made all the dog breeds, Americans see it as their job to preserve them all. To change a breed or adapt it to a new use is sacrilegious. In their view, at the right hand of God there is one perfect specimen of each

---

5 See the French-Canadian system of domesticating dogs (page 104) for a minority-supported method.

breed. The American dog breeder's goal is to have all the individual dogs in each breed look like God's perfect dogs. The breeders have written standards, which are guides to recognizing those perfect dogs. Breeders attend the sheepdog trials, the field dog trials, and the hunting dog trials, searching for dogs that may have escaped strict adherence to standards, and thus need improvement in their appearance. They are so passionate about their work that we have hardly any bad-looking dogs in America. And each year the high priests of the breed clubs look over all the dogs and pick the one that embodies perfection, entitling him to commit original sin with the dozens of slightly less than perfect dogs, thereby achieving an average improvement. This is no mean improvement on the German system (see pages 6–7). The goal of the American dog movement is to have all members of a breed look alike. How they act is not important.

✳   ✳   ✳

The first system of classifying hunting dogs was developed by the early Greeks who grouped dogs according to the four known basic elements: Earth, Air, Fire, and Water. Many dog-breeding hunters stuck to the Greek system and named their breeds after the medium in which the dogs worked. Thus you have dogs that hunt in the Water (the Chesapeake Bay Retriever, for example); in the Earth (terriers); in Fire (only the Dalmatian survives to the present, probably because it was wise enough to follow the fire truck rather than snuffling about in the flames); and, of course, the Airedale.

One modern way of classifying dogs is by their function. Hunting dogs whose names truly reflect their purpose include staghounds, foxhounds, wolfhounds, and lion hounds (these last are extremely rare). But sometimes the nomenclature within a class gets murky, and you quickly find you cannot rely on dogs' names to reveal accurately what their breeder had in mind. Take the terriers as an example. Terriers (the name comes from the Latin word for earth, *terra*, which surprised me because when I started this research I didn't know that hunters even knew Latin) go after prey in holes in the ground. The specialty of many terrier breeds is rodents, so they really should be called rodent terriers, in order to keep a certain consistency of terminology within the terrier group. For example, fox terriers go into a hole or underground den after a fox, so they are aptly named. Likewise, a foxhound avoids holes and looks specifically above the ground for specifically foxes.

But don't conclude that hound breeders, at least, have figured out how to name their breeds: think of truffle hounds. Their job is to dig into the ground for fancy mushrooms, and therefore they should be known as truffle terriers. If they specialized in *chasing* the mushrooms, then they could be called truffle hounds (compare also the greyhounds, which chase white metal rabbits).

Another system of classifying hunting dogs is by size. This differentiation often comes within a given breed. Poodles, for example, descended from an ancient and highly talented French duck-retrieving dog (the barbet), and are classified as standard (large), miniature (small), or toy (even smaller than that). Beagles, whose name supposedly means "to bay from the throat"[6] and which are noted for baying from the throat after rabbits, also come in different sizes. You can have the 15-inch (38-cm) beagle, the 10-inch (25.4-cm) beagle, or the small (9-mm) boar hound.

Still other hunting breeds have regional names—like Labrador retriever, Karelian bear dog, or Boston terrier—which writers often claim represent their place of origin. But the cognoscenti know that those are actually the only places where the dogs work, which is why you find them there.

And then there are dogs that people modestly named after themselves: the monks of St. Hubert developed the St. Hubert hound; the Reverend Jack Russell crafted his own terrier. Since they named the breeds after themselves, who knows what the dogs were supposed to do. It would not surprise me if many of you assume that the little Jack Russell terrier ran around looking in holes for His Reverence.

To further confuse the nomenclature issue, many hunting dogs perform tasks other than the one they were bred

---

6 "Beagle" is not related to "bugle," in spite of orthographic and sonorous similarities; "bugle" is apparently, and inexplicably, related to the Latin word for a baby ox, *buculus*.

for. Pointers can be trained to retrieve. It is easy to get bird retrievers to chase deer and deerhounds to hunt porcupines. My wife has a Chessie, a fine duck-retrieving dog, but the dog prefers to scarf blueberries. She (the dog) is a top-notch blueberry hunter. Unfortunately, she (my wife) cannot get her dog to "deliver to bucket," and most of the blueberries become dog. (The rest are useful for staining rugs.)

So really, unless you know the breed, you have no way of knowing, based on its name, what the dog does. Does the Kerry blue terrier's name indicate its emotional state? Is an Irish water dog supposed to fetch a chaser?

And how many of the remaining eighty-four breeds in my field guide to the dogs are fishing dogs? Only four. Fishing dogs are extremely quiet animals: it simply serves no useful function to bark in or under water, and therefore they do not come to the public's attention like the tree-bayers.

At any rate, the four breeds of fishing dogs that have managed to get listed in the field guide are really only token fishing dogs. The Portuguese water dog chases fish that get out of the nets of fishermen and brings them back. This commercial application generally bars them from sporting events. The Labrador retriever purportedly helps fishermen draw in nets, but nobody tells you they are mosquito nets. The beagles included in this group on the strength of its use "even for catching fish," but this assertion strikes me as a sales gimmick or hopeful afterthought. The only beagle I ever knew that caught fish was one that fell through the ice:

we found him the next summer full of eels. And, in Japan, the Kyūshū dog is noted as a "fisherman's helper." We'll see what that means in the section on bilge dogs.

There are actually many more fishing breeds, dogs which far outclass these four in piscatorial ability. Fishermen have always been interested in perfection, and they improve on what they have that is good, rather than casting about for new models. For that reason they have not saturated the field with dogs to the extent that hunters have. Any less-than-perfect fishing dogs are rigorously selected against, which is in stark contrast to hunting dogs, which simply get left home to keep the hearth warm if they don't work well. (You would never hear of a pike pointer, for example, getting stuck on a point.)

Hunters developed two kinds of dogs: helper dogs are typified by the old dog that drags himself to his feet when the hunting jacket comes off the peg and accompanies his master to the store for cigars; participatory dogs are primarily deer (or coon) chasers. Fishermen have also developed two types of dogs, both of which are unique to fishing. Gillie dogs are like tools: fishermen use them to increase their chances of hooking a fish. Fish spotter dogs actually participate in the fish, just as a pointer participates in the hunt. To simplify things (and because I can), I've chosen a classification system for the fishing dogs that is based on their function in relation to fishermen.

Introduction to
the Gillie Dogs

THE GILLIE DOGS ARE SIMPLY DOGS THAT HELP THE SPORTS fisherman. Within the gillie class there are two types: the baildales, which work inside the boat and which evolved from the ancestral bilge pups into the Pacific monsoon dog, the Greek gyro, and the various bowplunk dogs, including the storied Maine bow dog; and the already-bailedales, which do their work outside the boat and include such breeds as the log dog, the floating mat dog, the flounder-hounder, and the stringer spaniel.

But first, a little etymology. In Britain, a *gillie* (or *ghillie*) is a sportsman's helper. Long before inebriated sportsmen and other party-goers thought up the designated driver, the ancient Scots always designated a person who specialized in carrying their clan's chief across rivers on his back.[1]

---

1 This was not necessarily because the chief had been drinking the national liquor, but because he did not want to get his feet wet. He was (usually) not afraid of cold water: chiefs in the old days were very important people, and other people who were on their way to becoming important shot at them a lot. This meant chiefs had to wear their armor all the time, and it is not good to cross streams in full armor.

A ravine or narrow stream in Scottish is a *gill* or *ghill*. The carrier was the gillie, but the root of that word is *gille*, which comes from the Gaelic word *gille*, which means boy or lad. The carryee was simply known as Chief or, when in formal dress, Sir Chief. A good gillie would lift weights (e.g., toss the caber) in his off-hours to stay in shape, because over the years chiefs got bigger and bigger (we can determine this by comparing suits of armor from the past and the present). A good gillie would also practice keeping the chief's feet out of the water so his shoes wouldn't rust, and avoiding slimy rocks; it was very important not to drop the chief, and even little slips might warrant a cuff behind the ear.

Legend has it that once upon a time a chief was being carried across a nice gill and, spotting an early sea-run salmon, he asked his gillie to "holde ye stille, gille, that I might fishe the ghille fore ae whylle." It was this chief, sitting on the gillie's back, whipping the old horsehair back and forth, who gave the word *gillie* its modern meaning. Since then, the British have used the term to mean a sportsman's helper. You often see these gillies on Scottish riverbanks, dressed in tweeds (commonly, a three-piece woolen suit), tying flies to match the hatch for a gentleman dressed in waders, a waterproof woolen sweater, and a snappy little woolen cap, who is whipping flies at the end of a seven-weight line at passing salmon, which are on a spawning run and therefore not feeding.

BILGE PUPS

The oldest known breed of gillie dog is the bilge pup. The oldest unknown breed of dog of any kind, gillie or not, is also the bilge pup. Bilgies were the first functional breed (a breed that is useful for something), and were the direct ancestors of all other gillie dogs, both baildales and already-bailedales.

When I was researching bilge pups, I had a shocker. *Shocker* is a technical scholarly term: when you are researching something and discover something else, something unsuspected, that something else is a shocker. As you may have noticed, I try to bury my research shockers in the middle of paragraphs so only the most pedestrian of readers will note them. Here is the one for this paragraph: our ancestors ate dogs. It's too bad, but everybody's ancestors did it, unless somebody's ancestors (like turtles) were vegetarians all the way down. At first I thought I was misreading the ancient literature when I came across, "These marineating dogs would become available if someone needed a snack," or, "It is time to chow down." Often the references to dog eating are stated innocuously, even euphemistically, like, "Bilge pups went to sea in little vessels of their own," or, "Sushihounds [a Japanese bilge pup breed] helped with lunch." The eating of dogs is a sad fact, but it is also the cornerstone of the dogs' evolution, as we shall see.[2]

---

2 The reason we don't eat dogs anymore is that only the inedible ones survived long enough to reproduce. This is a wonderful example of Darwinian evolution in action: natural selection has favored the

The first written records of these ancient fishing dogs were in the log books of ancient Chinese fishing boats. Fishermen sailed out for extended periods, so they stowed lots of junk food down in the bilge, and it was there that they began breeding bilge pups in quantity. Junk chandleries were the original puppy mills. The Chinese were also the first to wok their dogs.

Sad fact or not, being eaten has changed many organisms into something useful. That is the basis of evolution. Bilge pups radiated into useful breeds in two distinct ways: 1) the evolutionary survivors were distasteful, and inedible, which gave them survival value and opportunities to be useful; 2) dogs that were pumped from the boat during bilging, or released during a shipwreck, were preadapted to already-bailedale conditions and floated effortlessly around the world, finally washing up on beaches and in bayous where there were not any people to eat them. Thus, for them, not being eaten is not a product of natural selection, but an acquired characteristic (see discussion about Lamarck, page 4).

The evolutionary problems for these washouts were staggering (remember "survival of the fittest") and it is a wonder that they have become so important in the advance-

---

smelliest breeds, which people would find repulsive to eat. If you don't believe this theory, test it by asking somebody if they would like chicken in a basset, or baked Alaska husky for supper. The immediate response will be, "that's disgusting." And I agree. I can't think of a single breed that is edible anymore—except maybe collieflower or German shepherd pie.

ment of new breeds. It is thought that the way to get really good dogs is to breed the best to the best, but there were no descendants of really good sushies. The most logical explanation is to assume that the ancients bred the worst to the worst, which accounts for many modern breeds.

Anyway, these bilge washouts evolved into the various breeds of already-bailedales, which we'll discuss later in this chapter.

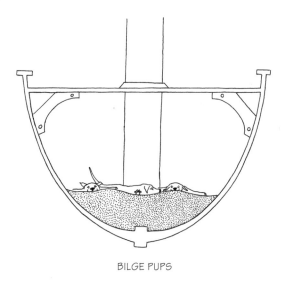

BILGE PUPS

Like so many breeds of dogs, bilge pups are named for the region they come from. Imagine for a minute the bilge of an ancient boat. My goodness, it must have been beautiful down in the dark oily depths of an ancient scow: a placid pool of carbon-based sludge enriched with nutritious gurries[3] and protected from the rough seas of the outside world. Here, in short, was the perfect evolutionary environment: rich in raw materials, climatically stable, and geographically isolated from the rest of the world. These are the ingredients for evolution. This is the place Darwin was looking for as he sailed around the globe in the good ship *Beagle*, in search of the origin of species. There it was, traveling along a few meters below him: the primordial soup of dogs—the *Beagle* is one of science's great ironies.

Over the years, of course, the bilge pups quietly evolved. Mostly, they changed color, developing the standard chocolate cream pie shade that typifies several modern dog breeds, both gillies and nonfishing working dogs.[4] The reason for this was not that ships' cooks preferred the flavor of chocolate-colored dogs—quite the contrary. When they reached into the dark bilge to get a dog for lunch, the lighter-colored, vanilla coated dogs naturally came first to the eye. Eventually the vanilla bilge pup population died out.

---

3 Gurry is fish offal, a highly descriptive term.

4 Chocolate is an example of what biologists call *cryptic coloration*: it blends in with its environment. Chocolate is so tasty that if it *could* be seen in the dark, it would be completely wiped out by now. This is why so many people trip over a chocolate lab in the dark. Those bilge pups that were conspicuous ended up investing all their energy in lunch programs and had none left for reproductive success. But colors like mocha fudge, coffee merle, walnut brindle, marbled pecan, and black-and-tan were not readily visible to ancient seafarers, which is why these bilge colors survived, and are so popular among dog fanciers today.

Thus the darker tops and lighter underneaths of the successfully adapted dogs exemplified the same principle as fish coloration (the dark color of the river bottom on top of the fish and the light color of the sky underneath). When the cook looked down into the dark hold, the dark upperside of the bilge pups was indistinguishable from the ship's bottom, whereas if the cook was under the dog looking up, the dog's bottom looked more like the sky looks if you're looking at it through bilge water. The next time you see a German shepherd's tan below, black above pattern, you'll know what I mean.

Because of this increasingly effective camouflage coloration, centuries passed when less and less was known about these hidden dogs in our lives. But evolution was taking place. It always does. You can't stop it. Aside from the dark color, another trait naturally selected was short legs: bilgies didn't need legs. They didn't need much of anything but a heads-up attitude and a buoyant disposition.

Baildales

As populations of bilge pups increased (ah, yes, there is sex in the bilge), competition (the battle of the bilge) for the little morsels from above might easily have led to a more aggressive, shark-like nature. Bilge pups could have developed pack behaviors homologous to those of their wolf ancestors—behaviors which, coupled with their aquatic lie-in-wait hunting techniques, they might have used to torpedo some unsuspecting merchant mariner who ventured into the bowels of the ship and, inevitably, into the bowels of the dogs. But these are just dogs and dogs have to be taught to be mean. All dogs are innately cuddly.[1]

Besides, these bilge pups were survivors. To eat an ancient mariner would be to the dog's disadvantage: who would sail the ship? Their emerging and mutually beneficial symbiotic relationship with man was centered around keeping the bilge clean. Well, not exactly clean, but different and better. Eventually they became gillie dogs. The helping behaviors the bilge pups perfected involved getting water

---

1 I don't know why bilge pups never became popular as pets, and since they don't actually do anything, neither do I understand why they haven't been registered with the AKC.

out of the boat, thus the category name of these modern gillie breeds: bail(s)dale(s).[2]

*Baildale*s are a general functional category, which can be compared with other differentiations of dogs such as the working or sporting dogs. Each of these categories is divided into subgroups, which are again subdivided. For example, one subgroup of the category working dogs is the sheepdogs, which comprise the conducting dogs (dogs that chase sheep from place to place) and the nonconducting sheepdogs (dogs that lie around the farm and bark a lot). In each of these subgroups there are several breeds; e.g., border collies, Great Pyrenees, and Catahoula leopardcowhog dogs.[3] Within the baildale category are subgroups, all of which we think are descended from the ancient bilgies. They have one trait in common: they all gillie from inside the boat. Later I will contrast them with the already-bailedales that also descended from the bilge pups, but they gillie from outside the boat.

---

2 Etymological note: breeders of baildales have split into different camps over a linguistic point. Some use the plural *bailsdale*, while others (like me) anglicize the word by simply adding an *s*, thus *baildales*. Still others adopt the Hungarian plural and write baildailok (dropping the final *e* and inserting the pluralizing *ok*), the way komondor(ok) and kuvasz(ok) breeders do (but then journalists, with great logic but little Hungarian orthographic knowledge, call them komondoroks and kuvaszoks, which is a double plural, and I don't think the AKC accepts such hybrids, which is okay by me).

3 Just because you never heard of Catahoula leopardcowhog dogs doesn't mean the breed doesn't exist. Look it up.

First, let's look at why baildale behavior was needed. Early fishermen used the waterlog, a style of boat that actually got better with age. After many years in the water, the internal portion of the log would rot away, leaving only the bark. Since they were already saturated, waterlogs were the only vessel ever invented that didn't leak. Still, they evolved, eventually, into the canoe, and the evolution of the canoe was simultaneous with that of the leak. Since then, the leak has become standard equipment on all boats.

With the perfection of the leak, boats were increasingly able to ship water.[4] Boat owners who shipped too much water were selected against, and so, naturally, were their bilge pups. I'm sure you can see where this is going: any mutations that led to the survival of boating humans also led to the survival of boating dogs. Most of the time, these symbiotic mutations were the responsibility of the dogs, which developed two methodologies: monsooning, which rids the boat of excess water; and ballasting, which prevents the boat owner from bringing in too much water. As time went on, each behavior led to specialization of tasks, and two main sub-subgroups of baildales evolved: the monsoon dogs and the ballast dogs.

---

4 Shipping water is a nautical expression meaning to take water from one place to another by boat.

MONSOON DOGS

The most famous baildale is the monsoon dog. These dogs achieved a brilliant mutation. The resulting monsoon gene imparts a functional behavioral perfection to this breed that was highly valued by mariners through the ages, so much so that these genes were dispersed throughout the whole dog world and are now virtually ubiquitous, albeit vestigial, in hunting and other nonworking breeds.

MONSOON DOG IN ACTION

Monsoon dogs lie in the bilge of a boat until they are disturbed by the shipping of water. When the water reaches nose level, which is their high water mark, the dog instinctively rises up out of the bilge (think about the creature from the lost lagoon) and unleashes with tremendous power a series of epicentric rotational reciprocations, expelling boat-threatening waters overboard.

Monsooner Standards

Once, dogs had hair all around their bodies, but this is a fault in the monsoon breed. (Water absorbed by chest and belly hair simply goes back into the boat during reciprocations, which is energetically inefficient.) Careful breeding and natural selection among the original monsooners favored dogs with little or no abdominal hair; also, the hairless stomach characteristic of most modern dogs is vestigial, meaning that if you look at your dog's tummy you won't see any hair and you won't know why (unless you've read this book).

Certain passages in ancient literature seem to imply that the original monsoon dogs could rid a boat of five ewers of water in a single shake. Field trial records are, unfortunately, unavailable, having been lost (or perhaps stolen by disgruntled breed club secretaries). It is an age-old tradition in dog breeding to lose the breed records, so the dogs' attributes live on in delightfully unreliable oral traditions and dog breeds attain a status closely supported by cultural mythology. And thus we may have slightly exaggerated standards for a "good" monsoon dog.

However, a bad monsoon dog is truly not worth having. The difference between a good monsooner and a bad one lies in its size; in the absorptive quality of the coat; in the dog's kinetic potential for reversing the torque of its skin; and, most critically, in its orientation abilities. Fine working monsoon dogs *always* align their nose-tail axis parallel to the stem-stern axis of the boat, while unacceptable dogs stand transverse to the operational direction of the boat, and abaft the beam. This latter position not only does not decrease the amount of water in the boat but it also places the dog squarely in front of the person at the tiller, with highly unsatisfactory results. (However, abaft-the-beam dogs make up most of our wonderful pets, and random selection of almost any registered dog will get you one of these magnificent dogs, with its misoriented monsooning still intact.)

When you buy a monsooner it is very, very important to choose a dog that will match the freeboard of your boat. If the dog is too tall (or will grow to be too tall), that is, if its nose is higher than the gunwale, then the dog won't start monsooning until you have shipped too much water. Natural selection will operate to eliminate you and your too-tall dog, so it is best to register too-tall dogs before they do much harm. Do keep in mind that too-short dogs have their own problem. Monsooning below the level of the gunwale just redistributes the water around inside the boat and, withal, makes it harder to see where you are going.

As I mentioned earlier, monsooners are ancient dogs

and passed along many traits to modern dogs that have never seen the inside of a boat. Fishermen only rewarded monsooning behavior that was displayed in the presence of people, mostly because it has never been wise to let a dog go fishing alone in a boat. In modern dogs this genetically programmed oscillatory behavior still needs the physical proximity of a person to elicit the response. My son Tigger's highly bred Chessies will wait, no matter how much they are suffering from waterloggedness, until you admit them into the house, and only there and in the presence of residents do they perform this otherwise highly desirable behavior of expelling scummy swamp water from their coats.

Dogs with the furry above/hairless below configuration sought in monsooners, and with strong oscillatory inclinations, tend to spray dog water on walls and ceiling instead of on the floor where it is easier to clean up. Many wives have adapted to bilge-colored ceilings. What we need to do now is select a dog that has hair on its tummy and nowhere else—perhaps a modified Mexican hairless breed, which, regardless of their rotational reciprocations, just dribble. Then all the water would end up on the floor, and none would soak the walls and ceiling and you, except for perhaps your shoes, which may need oiling anyway. While we wait for this new dog to evolve, I suggest you keep a towel rack by the door like we do. Or hire your dogs out to tropical gardens, where they can be useful in recreating tropical rainforest atmospheres.

Ballast Dogs

All through history, due to the nature of their jobs, the bilgies and monsooners have walked a waterline between life and death. It is not surprising that natural selection has favored the more stable ballast dog.

Ballast dogs are blue-blooded descendants of the bilge pups. Starting in the depths of shipping, they gradually traded positions, learning to counter the instabilities of the present for the securities of the future. So whenever their vessel started to tip dangerously, they abandoned their downward position, moving to the other (up) side, immediately increasing their chances for survival. This bullish behavior leveraged cargo weight to the highs, countervailing the lows. Level boats are always a big selective advantage, and people and dogs who make them that way are the real winners. Over the centuries, the ballast dogs have sub-sub-subdivided into the stalwart bowplunk breeds and the more athletic gyro dogs.

Bowplunk Dogs

One of the more famous American ballast dogs is the bowplunk dog known as the Maine bow dog. This breed was originally recognized by Mr. Barnaby Porter of Damariscotta, Maine. With his kind permission, his breed standard is printed here for the first time, though I'm sure such a fine description has probably been printed in other places for the first time too.

Observations on the Maine Bow Dog
by Barnaby Porter

It's time the Maine coon cat was put in its place. It has been highly overrated as a breed all these years, and I'm not so sure anyone has a true and accurate idea of just what makes a coon cat a coon cat anyhow. It's an appellation that has come to have about as much meaning as "colonial farmhouse." Rather common-looking balls of fluff are what they are.

Of much more convincing pedigree is a hardy and noble breed of dog, heretofore not made much of because of its humble beginnings and conspicuous absence from the show ring. This is the magnificent Maine Bow Dog, his name deriving from his deeply ingrained habit of standing, proud and brave, on the bow of his master's boat as it plies the lively waters along the Maine coast.

There is nothing quite so moving as the sight of such a dog holding his station, ears flying and a big smile on his face, as his sturdy vessel bounds over the sparking whitecaps, his profile emblazoned on the horizon.

The points of conformation in the Bow Dog breed are far from strict. The dog's size, color and general appearance have nothing to do with it. Even pom pom tails are allowed. Good claws are the only mandatory physical attribute. It's mostly a matter of character and carriage. The animal must have superb footing and balance, and most important, he must display the eagerness and bravery of the true Bow Dog. A passion for boats and the water is essential, for the dog must be willing and able to maintain the classic stance, chin up and chest out, in even gale force winds.

Individual Bow Dogs may vary greatly in style, but their dedication to duty must be unquestionable. One I know, named "Wontese," who looks something like a Springer Spaniel, is such a glutton for cold and punishing duty that his uncontrolled but enthusiastic chattering has become legendary. Another, named "Duke," wears a sou'wester. Remarkable, these dogs.

Being in the Working Dog class, Bow Dogs are permitted the occasional slipup to be expected in the real world conditions under which they must perform. Mine, an almost flawless specimen, was most embarrassed one day when he broke stance for a brief moment to take a flea break. There was a blustery chop on the sea, and in a flash, he slipped ingloriously over the side, his gleaming claws raking the bow as he disappeared from sight. A valuable dog like that, I had to come around and fish him out of the w es. I hoisted his drenched bulk back aboard, and without so much as a thought about shaking off, he leaped up forward to where he belonged, brave and proud, ears flying.

*That's a Maine Bow Dog if I've ever seen one. It made
me proud to be his master.*

Mr. Porter obviously knows his dogs, and he does a
good job of reporting on the courage and nobility of this
breed, which stands in the bows of fishing boats and looks
good no matter what—even though there is great variability
in the way they look. (This is lucky, however, because there
is a similar variability in the looks of Maine fishing boats and
even greater variability in the looks of Maine fishermen.
Matching bow dog to boat should not be the problem it is
with the baildales.) Mr. Porter seems unaware that his dog
belongs to a functional breed classically known as the ballast dog, and though he does realize that the breed is highly
functional, he misses the connection between the dog's
function and its "conspicuous absence from the show ring,"
since it is not registered with any kennel club in the world,
so far as I know.

The purpose of a ballast dog standing in the bow (the
front, or pointy end of the boat) is to hold it down in the
water while you paddle or steer from the stern. (The reason
it is called the "stern" is because it is a very serious part of
the boat, being where you hang the outboard motor, and
steer from.) Trolling (named after the character who fished
under bridges when you were a kid) also takes place in the
stern. Really good bow dogs have an innate sense of "trim."
As the speed of the boat increases, the dog leans farther and
farther forward, keeping the boat "trimmed," or relatively
even in the water.

FISHERMAN WITHOUT BOWPLUNK DOG

FISHERMAN WITH BOWPLUNK DOG

Mr. Porter was on the right track when he listed the problem areas in Maine bow dogs. He correctly points out that they should be agile, as well as able to concentrate for long periods of time and avoid fleeting distractions. This means a good Maine bow dog really ought not fall overboard. Natural selection would have taken care of this problem years ago, if only fishermen would just keep going and tend to business instead of forgiving a fallen dog. But the dog is half of a closely-bonded team, and that attachment is rarely ruptured just because one member of the party made a mistake. Very few fishermen have the sheer Darwinian courage not to turn back in an attempt to rescue a fallen bow wow, and this prevailing softheartedness has been a large factor in the dog's morphology: a successful bow dog has a hefty scruff.

Scruffs[5] were an early adaptation in this breed, developed even before the perfection of bowplunk behavior. And it's easy to see why. When a stabilizing bowplunk dog goes overboard in heavy seas, the danger of capsizing is doubly great: leaning over the side and grabbing a struggling dog by the scruff of its neck can be a selective disadvantage for both symbionts.

However, scruffs do have a disagreeable side effect when combined with monsooning behavior. Monsooning is, for the Maine bow dog, vestigio-functionless (to use the technical term). After the dog's unplanned baptism and resurrection (and only in the immediate proximity of a human), its preprogrammed, metronomic monsooning behavior is unleashed. And, of course, because no one has ever thought to breed good monsooners (see page 24) with good bow dogs (see Mr. Porter's description, above), this syncopated shiver and splatter is never displayed in the bowplunk position (forward in the bow), but rather in the stern of the boat where the central axis of the dog is abaft the beam and upwind. Mr. Porter's dog is the only one I have ever heard of that skipped what he calls "shaking off" and went right back to his post. But the mere fact that he mentioned it suggests that he might be fibulating.

---

5 The famous British dog show is named after this organ.

In the absence of a monsooner × bow dog cross-breed, training a substitute behavior in your bow dog is nearly impossible. And, of course, trimming the scruff is highly unethical (as well as dangerous). Reward and punishment models are tough to effect: many times I have stood in the athwart position with a large stick (two-by-four), ready to demonstrate disapproval, only to be thrown off by a vigorous monsoon. And, the one time I actually tried to make an impact on the dog, I clobbered myself on the fulcrum part of my left sea leg.

Gyro Dogs

The gyro dog was derived during ancient fishing days, when boats were really tippy. Back then, the boat builders' union agreed (this time with each other) to make all boats tippy. The old ship builders were so good that boats would and could last forever—unless they sank. Leaks might have done the trick, but monsooners were invented, so ship builders went to tippy canoes. Marine architects began designing in instability as a kind of planned obsolescence.[6] Encouraged by their guild, producers and designers thereby kept production at a maximum while still crafting seemingly good quality boats.

---

6 Stan says this was maybe the only time in economic history when union and management worked to mutual benefit.

Lost in the mist nets of antiquity is the story of how fishermen came up with the idea of separate but equally weighted dogs to counterbalance their tippy bateaux. The gyro dog is my favorite, using the same gimbalic principle of the gyro compass, with an organic difference. The dog simply goes to the opposite side of the boat from the fisherman. This counterbalances the fishing activities.

Not lost in the mists of antiquity is the authentication of Greek gyro dogs as the first examples of purebred, function-specific ballast dogs. Marco Polo, returning from China to the Mediterranean world, is said to have brought with him the ancestors of these dogs—bilge pups, of course—along with other curiosities like spaghetti. The Greeks developed the best gyros.

What happened was, Greek fishermen found that around lunchtime these bilgies had a tendency to go to the opposite side of the boat from the fisherman. This was natural to them, given their origins as the world's first junk food. As the fishermen chased the dogs around the boat, the boat stayed level. Eureka! Several dialogues later, the next logical question arose: how could you get the boat to stay level during the *non*-prelunch periods?

The Greeks developed two solutions to the tippy problem, both of which are still used. The first solution was simply to lunch all the time. (Stan's a champion at this, dragging out the prebreakfast period, during which our boat is always level because nobody is in it for most of the morning, and so no fishing is going on, and subsequently, he's trying to find where he stowed the ingredients for lunch, which worries me as well as the dog.)

The second solution was to wear a mask on the back of the head with a fierce, hungry-looking face on it. It was a matter of simple Skinnerian conditioning to elicit the dog's "180 degrees away" motion in reaction to the mask. Primary conditioning was accomplished with the fisherman facing the dog, using his own face to show how hungry he was. Once the dog was conditioned to move away from this expression, the fisherman wore the hungry face on the back of his head, thus maintaining the boat's delicate balance at all times. The resulting breed was the Greek gyro. Once perfected, many of these gyros became real heroes.[7]

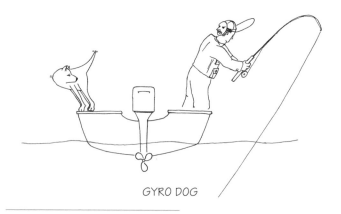

GYRO DOG

7 I should point out that one school of anthropology credits the gyros to the Sub-Sandwich Islanders. See "anthropologists agree" footnote, page 1.

In tippy fishing boats, balance is everything. With a good fighting bluefish skiffing about, now on this side, now on that, a good gyro dog will just about run himself to death trying to stay opposite the fisherman. If you use these dogs, remember that it is important to keep the boat free of treble hooks and other debris. Not only are sharp pointy little things hazardous for the dog, but if the dog has to jump over them, his counterbalancing weight appears and disappears from the surface of the boat, causing a dangerous oscillation (technically known as a gyration). A really top-notch gyro will keep one foot on the deck of the boat at all times, correcting any oscillations created by herself or the fisherman.

Before you invest in a gyro, take it out for a test-fish—or at least watch how it reacts to your hungry-face. Stanley had this one dog he named Hoagie. Nice dog, but totally unsuitable for fishing. This dog was afraid of nothing—which as you may guess is a fault in this breed: good gyros are innately afraid of being eaten. But Hoagie actually looked forward to breakfast. He did his share of the work by doing the dishes every morning, and sometimes he gave them another swipe when we got back in the evening. He was very good at getting the little lumps off the bottom of the frying pan. Next thing though, Stanley got the dog interested in fishing. Disaster. Right in the middle of the excitement the darn dog would come over to see if you were catching a keeper for supper.

Already-Bailedales

THE GILLIE DOGS WHO REALLY GO OVERBOARD ARE THE already-bailedales, including the stringer spaniels and the noblest of the gillie dogs, for my money, the floating mat dogs.

FLOATING MAT DOGS

Floating mat dogs are the elite among fishing dogs. They are the cleverest, the most fun to work with, and they make the best house dogs I know. They don't chase cats or cars. They don't have that in-and-out-all-the-time behavior. For the most part, you can put a floating mat dog anywhere and it is no more trouble than the average scatter rug. Once in a while it's good to vacuum them.

Out in the field, they assist in a variety of ways. Since, like all dogs, they are waterproof, and fur is a good insulator, they can be draped over minnow pails when the sun is hot, or over lunch bags on rainy days. (In lunch bag situations, it's wise to keep the head end of the dog away from the soft parts of the lunch.) The first fishing dog I ever had was a floating mat dog.

Years ago, shortly before our trial separation, Stan and I began going to Ontario to fish. We usually went every fall, just before school opened, to get our heads straight before we had to go back to work. Our quarry was northern pike. For those of you who are just interested in dogs and don't know much about fishing, you have to understand that fall fishing for pike consists mostly of casting into weeds and snags. This was the first method I'd learned, and Stan taught it to me. It is the standard method of catching August "hammer-handle" pike.

One year we changed our routine slightly, so that as soon as school was over in the spring we headed north. This got our heads straighter earlier, and we figured we could still go again in August. But the real reason for the May foray was to catch big pike. You catch big pike just after ice-out. Spring fishing for humongous pike is in the flats or where they cruise along rocky shores or windswept points, or on the edge of the ice, or maybe in deep holes or at the mouths of little streams. You fish anywhere except under weeds. That's because there are no weeds in the spring. That's because weeds haven't grown up yet. That's because the water isn't warm enough for weeds yet, and because the ice hasn't uncovered the weeds yet, and for a thousand other reasons, including that Mother Nature doesn't like weeds in the spring.

Our problem was Stan, bless his heart. Talk about trying to teach an old dog new tricks. (In fact I've learned a lot about training dogs from watching Stan.) When you're fishing for pike with Stan you're casting to weeds or lily pads. That is the way to fish for pike, according to Stan. He is dogmatic about this. That is the way we did it on the Mattagami and the Kapuskasing Rivers. That is the way we always caught pike and so there is no other way.

"Stan," I said one day, "let's troll a rocky windswept point."

He looked at me as if I were stupid. "You can't find weeds on a rocky windswept point," he said, patiently. So off we went, scraping the bottom of the boat, and the propeller, in shallows that would have pike grass in two months. The lone lily pad was still shivering so hard it would scare the pike. But there was no arguing with Stan and we floated around in the little bays like Sir John Franklin looking for the Northwest Passage.

That summer was when we tried the trial separation, and our therapist talked us into getting a dog in order to give our relationship more stability. She thought if we could focus on someone else's needs rather than being selfishly anchored to invisible weed beds, it might ease the tension.

So I did the research, Stan chipped in his half, and by the next year's ice-out we had this amazing dog, our first floating mat dog. We were so happy. Not only did he give us something to take care of besides ourselves, but we could use him in the spring to simulate the floating mats of weeds that we needed to cast to. Stan called the pup Mat, which I thought was pretty unimaginative. I bet half the dogs in the Floating Mat Dog Association are named Mat: Doormat, Welcome Mat, Automat, Big Mat, and Matilda. (Other people with floating mat dogs name them after some specific kind of floating vegetation like Lily Pad, or Hyacinth, and once in a while you'll get a Sargasso, or just plain Scum. One of my cleverer colleagues, a marine ecologist, named her mat dog Phytoplankton, or Phyto for short.) When I mentioned the lack of imagination issue to Stan in a nice way, he said the name was short for Matthew and he always wanted a dog named Matthew. That confused me because if he wanted a dog named Matthew why would he call him Mat? Why not do the yuppie bit and call him Thew? It just didn't make sense, but since I was trying to make this relationship work, I let it go and we both began using the affectionate form, "Matty."

Floating Mat Dog Evolution

The first use of a mat dog for fishing probably happened in Florida in the late nineteenth century. The original stock was bilge pups of the monsoon strain, which came ashore when some Spanish galleon sank. For a while the conquistadors used the dogs as saddle blankets for their ponies but they ended up like most horse products—strewn around the yard, unnoticed for years.

Now, in Florida there has been a long tradition of cleaning the yard by throwing everything into the lake. Some

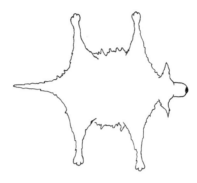

FLOATING MAT DOG (PLAN VIEW)

fisherman (mowing the lawn) must have chucked one of those old bilge pup remnants into the pond, where it floated. Fish swam under the shadow, using it the same way they use overhanging rocks or weeds.

Fish like shady places. Fish stuck in the middle of a pond would have as much trouble with ozone holes as we do. Fish in bright light are seen more easily by birds and become vulnerable to predation. Little fish having this problem hide in shadows and big fish trying to eat little fish hide in the same shadows, while male fish looking for lovers hide in the shadows because that is where female fish will be finding food to make eggs. Many of life's strategies take place in the shadows. This is why you cast to lily pads and logs. It is well known that fish don't like bright light, but it is not so well known that in most ponds there is not enough shade for everybody. Shade is an "ecological limiting factor,"

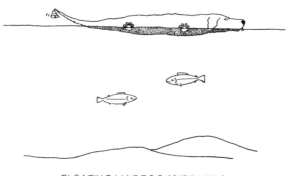

FLOATING MAT DOG (SIDE VIEW)

which means that there might not be enough shade for all those fish that require shade. And it is this situation that the fisherman and his mat dog exploit.

A group of Florida fishermen, known affectionately to each other as "Crackers," had the same problem. These Saltines, who fished offshore, fathomed that out in the Atlantic Ocean there is the same amount of shade as in the middle of the Sahara Desert. Realizing that you can't find fish in the middle of the Sahara, they searched for shade and found it under the manta rays. Under these slowly gliding tarpaulins all the fish in the world are stacked up, each trying to get a little drift of shadow. Even pelicans know this trick, and raft together.

The Saltines are pretty smart Cookies, so they thought they would get a manta mimic. One of them (a fisherman on temporary lawn-mowing duty) had a dog that looked like a tangle of lily pads, which his wife used to cover a bare spot in the lawn. If he could get it to act like a bunch of lily pads in a backwater, his fishing future would be assured.

Kazaam! Those lily pad/weed mimics were all over the backyards of Florida: dogs with lots of stringy hair with things growing in it. Flat, motionless dogs with quiet but uplifting personalities. Dogs that had spent generations collecting shade waiting for the time to give some back. Here were dogs foreshadowing a revolution in evolution: preadapted slough-hole yard-dogs become floating mat dogs—a useful and valuable breed. This was evolution without change, something every conservationist dreams of.

The floating mat dogs instantly achieved behavioral perfection. They still exhibit all the same behaviors while floating in a bayou, pond, or lake that their ancestors did on a sultry afternoon when the burglars arrived. These may not be the kind of dog that would jump into a pickup truck (or even jump out of one), but when you get to the lake and float one, it is a pure thrill to watch it in inaction.

Training And Fishing Your Mat Dog

Because I'm the biologist, I got to raise and train Matty over that first winter. Training is not hard, because basically the floating mat dog will just float on the water wherever you leave it. Find a fishing area in at least four to six feet of water and gently slip the mat dog over the side, allowing its hair to fully spread out over the water. The dog's legs should

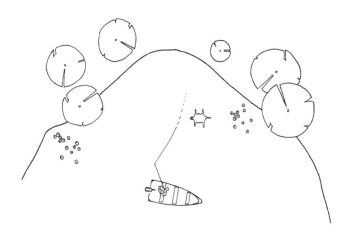

FLOATING MAT DOG (AERIAL VIEW)

extend out along with the hair and be held in a quarterly pattern.

That's it. You can increase your mat dog's value by training it to take an active interest in the sport so that it watches underneath itself and gently raises its tail when a legal-sized fish is present. A bell on its tail helps to rouse a drowsy fisherman.

Matty got the hang of his job right off and started to embellish. He would mimic all kinds of vegetation. His best was eel grass: the first time I saw his eel grass I thought he was just cold, but what he was doing was raising his hair above the water and letting it bend slightly in the wind. What artistry! It looked so natural, the way the hair would tip and then shake slightly just as if a little breeze had come along. One morning I could have sworn I saw a floating basket with a little Moses, but it was just Matty, trying out another image.

Longhaired mat dogs can't swim very well because the spread-out legs get tangled in the tresses. Thus, when the wind is blowing (not a problem in the early morning, before breakfast) or currents are brisk, Stan and I recommend anchoring the dog by its collar. If there is too much wind or current, then a belt around the dog's waist allows it to drift headfirst, downwind or down current. The anchor rope should be at least three times the depth of the water, as a rope that is too short will cause the dog's head to be pulled below the surface, causing an unnecessary commotion and scaring the fish.

The secret is to get the drift right. Gently pitch a dog out to a strategic location, and you'll have the time of your life. Mud and other debris that are naturally tangled in the dog's coat are an advantage, making him appear more authentic. Insects buzzing around a mat dog are usually plentiful, probably because the moisture balance in the hair is conducive to the growth and reproduction of pesky six-leggers. Their regular appearance at the periphery of the working mat dog is an aid in attracting the feeding fish. There is no "matching the hatch" problem with a well-unkempt floating mat dog.

Casting to a floating dog mat should be done carefully. You have to cast over the dog, letting the lure drift off slightly with the wind. This way the retrieve won't snag the dog. It is especially important not to snag especially young dogs because you can easily sour them on fishing. They begin to flinch as you cast to them, scaring the fish below. Spinner baits work well but buzz baits tickle, forcing the dog into compulsive scratching, which, again, scares the fish.

At noon the shadow is directly below the dog, but it varies with time of day and season, and you will have to adjust your casting. Try to cast to the shadow side of the dog, west in the morning and east in the afternoon if you're in the northern hemisphere. This keeps your hook closer to the fish. Be aware of the wind, because it can affect your cast. You need to adjust your boat to the wind and to the shadow angle, always mindful of the hook/dog relationship.

Before you float a mat dog, remove all the shiny metal tags from its collar. Many top-level toothy piscivorous fish (pike and muskies are good examples) can't tell the difference between a rabies tag and a silver spoon. I once had a pike strike savagely at a dog tag and try to swim off with my dog. This is another good way to sour a dog.

For nearly the same reason, I prefer female mat dogs. Their profile in the water is smoother and nothing hangs down to attract snacking fish. Older male dogs can get nervous in muskie country and that nervousness gets passed on to the fisherman, making the cast rate go way up.

Floating mat dogs are tough to exercise in the off season. I tried leaving one in a nearby pond while I went to work, but an early freeze-up discouraged me from doing that again. Many are too big for the bathtub, and my wife objects to using the swimming pool if they are shedding. But letting your mat dog get out of shape can be disastrous: you'll find that the first time you use it in the spring, the skin will wrinkle and crack (and, of course, leak).

So far there are no laws about how many mat dogs you can use, but the time surely will come. Some fishermen attach a small flag to the dog's tail so it looks like a tip-up for ice fishing. While this is certainly an aid when you are using ten or more dogs, I feel this practice may lead to laws that equate the dogs to mechanical devices, and their use will be restricted to six or seven dogs at any one time. Legislation has already been drafted in England to prevent the floating of many dogs, although mat dogs are popular there. The British seem to prefer dogs that don't do anything and these dogs are naturals at that. Also, you can fish them at any time of day, which is good for both mat dogs and Englishmen.

Choosing a Mat Dog

I like brown mat dogs with some water lily–yellow streaking. Recently, several people have reported good luck with black dogs. Green would be best, but my geneticist friends say green is impossible to select for in a dog. The rare white mat dog can be dyed green, but this is expensive as not many grooming parlors carry green in sizes larger than a toy poodle.[1]

Conformation is very important in floating mat dogs. Seen from above, the good ones have an almost perfectly round appearance when floating on a pond. From a side view, however, they are almost flat. This flatness gives added surface area and therefore shadow, and also means they pack well. Some fishermen just roll them up and store them in PVC pipes on the roof of the van.

As for old Matty, disaster eventually struck our faithful first mat dog. I really can't blame it all on Stan. Stan hadn't noticed that I'd put Matty in the van, and he piled all the gear on him. I think it was all those plastic milk crates full of frying pans and other kitchen paraphernalia that did him in. So help me we never gave it a thought until we were unloading at the float plane. When we discovered Matty on the bed of the van, we suspected the worst, but given the true-to-breed nature and conformation of the dog it was difficult to tell how bad it was. We decided to give him the benefit of the doubt and fished him. He seemed to do pretty well for a couple of days before it got pretty clear that his sole was in a different plaice. This was no fluke. He was dead. It is now many years later and we have a kennel full of

1 Some Chessies are supposed to be a "dead grass" color, and that is not very different from "peat bog." At least the Chessies my son has are very close to that color, especially when they are lying on the dining room rug. It is one of those mysteries of evolution, where the background of an animal's preferred habitat begins to look like the animal. In just a few short years all our rugs have taken on a dead grass color.

floating mats, but we always remember that Matthew came first. He was a true fisher among dogs.

FLOUNDERHOUNDERS

Imperfection is what evolution is all about, and that's as true for dogs as it is for fishing buddies. But, since the beginning of time, breeders have capitalized on imperfection. If that weren't the case we wouldn't have the dogs we do today.

Breeders of purebred dogs are people who preserve nature's major anomalies. How else could they have turned the dog morphologically into the most varied species in the world? When man came along the natural world was full. There was a species in every niche. Nothing more could happen. But dog breeders discovered a way to put some life into modern evolution: adaptation is passé; maladaption is au courant. Strive not for perfection of form, but take tiny maladaptive characteristics and perfect them. For example, clever breeders have perfected the snore. Breeds like the Boston terrier and English bulldog may not be able to do anything else well, but they can snore better than any creature on earth. Hungarian breeders have perfected the coats on their dogs so nothing can get through it except some specialized smells. The puli and the komondor have such perfect coats that you can't even get a snarl out.

If the wolf could only have known what it was coming to. Just when you think breeders have separated all the different conformations, shapes, sizes, and colors into separate breeds, along comes the flounderhounder. The flounder-hounder is the most striking of all the dog anomalies.

This is not my favorite breed of dog, and I don't recommend them as working dogs. But since I'm trying to be compleat and give the reader the whole picture of this gillie dog world I feel obligated to include the flounderhounder.

Some time ago, there was found in Louisiana a variety of the old bilge dogs that were so lazy they must have lain on their self-same side throughout evolutionary history. One eye, usually the left, has migrated to the right side of the head, so the dog has two eyes on that side. The migration of the eye wasn't noticed for a long time, which is understandable under the circumstances.

In the early evolutionary period of the eye (the paleolidics), the dog's left eye was in the down position, looking directly into the lawn. Because it was geologically a very damp period, the dog often kept the eye shut tightly, but of course even a tight eyelid can still leak. Thus natural selection favored those dogs whose eyelids grew shut, giving the dog a leakless disposition, and preventing any foreign substances whatsoever from infecting the eyeball.

By keeping such a tight lid on, the down eye couldn't see. But this wasn't really a selective disadvantage because it couldn't see very far into the lawn anyway.[2] Another reason

---

2 The eyes of several other dog breeds are also vestigial: for example, the breeds with the hanging gardens of Babylon covering their faces (see Hungarian dogs, above, and Olde Englishe Sheepe Dogges, chapter one), so that nothing including light is allowed to get through to the dog.

these dogs couldn't see well was that they were mostly asleep.[3]

Throughout the mesolidic eye-evolution process, the vestigial eye went looking for something to do. It migrated through the head. This developmental process, like all evolutionary advancements, had to be done very slowly. This was not because there were obstacles to the migration, but rather because it didn't know where to go. For a long period of time, while the eye was in the middle of the head (halfway between where it was in ancestral times and where it ended up in descendent times[4]), nobody noticed that the dog didn't have an eye on the down side.

Next came the neolidic period of the flounderhounder's development, popularly known as the Cajun Surprise. One day a bayou buster went to feed the dog and the dog was looking at him with two eyes. As always the dog looked pleased with himself and wagged his tail.

---

3 Sleep is an energy-saving behavior perfected by dogs. Scientists have not found any other species that conserves as much energy as the domestic dog. Conservationists have nominated the dog for a sustainable-energy award.

4 Descendent may be a confusing term because the eye was moving up or ascending. Ascendent might be a better word since this is an evolutionary advancement: the ancestral form and the ascendent form. Humans are the only real descendants because they came down out of the trees. Technically, domestication cannot be either an ascent or descent because it is an unnatural selection—especially where the dog is concerned.

Zappo! The guy becomes an instant expert dog breeder on the basis of this one dog with both eyes on the same side. This is not unusual for dog breeders. They discover that there is something different about their dog and presto! They start another breed. Technically they are giving the dog "a sporting chance." Why waste time breeding the best to the best in some slow evolutionary fashion when you could put a little English on it? Besides, breeding the best to the best in dogs means breeding the best looking ones, and for flounderhounders the best looking ones had both eyes on the same side of the head.

Once this one-sided looking behavior was discovered, it was thought that the dog might be preadapted to specialized work. Breeders first tried fishing the dog for flounder (if it looked like one, it should act like one). This is the single instance in the dog world where function followed looks.

Flounderhounders tend to be flatter than mat dogs, because people in Louisiana tend to mow their lawns. Therefore they have very little lung capacity, and tend to sink. Breeders theorized if they had small lungs it was an adaptation to not needing air, just like the bulldog people selected for nose plugs in their dogs because they only need air to snore with. Next, since the dog sinks to the bottom of the lake, they thought it was adapted to lying on the bottom pretending to be a flounder.

Some saw this as an alternative to the floating mat dog. Instead of spreading the shadow from the top of the water (as a floating mat does), where the shadow gets diffused by light leaking from the sides, the flounderhounder, lying directly on the bottom, has the best quality shadow of any of the already-bailedales. I don't find this particularly useful, actually, because even though the shadow is superbly dark, the dog doesn't cast enough of it. The total volume of shadow can be calculated by multiplying the surface area of dog by the depth of the water under the dog. Therefore, a three-foot diameter (93 cm) mat dog in four feet (113.5 cm) of water gives 28.3 cubic feet (6793 cubic cm) of shade. The same sized flounderhounder settling to the bottom would give you seven square feet (and zero cubic feet) of shade. And why would you want a dog with seven square feet?

The breed's lack of lung capacity is actually an adaptation to long periods of dormancy. As a front dormancy, flounderhounders make nice welcome mats, wagging their tails but not leaping up to paw or sniff. They are easy to store in the off season, and many people use flounderhounders as scatter rugs. But don't try to fish one. No matter what the breeders tell you they do need air. The best you can do is use them in the intertidal flat, but only when the tide is out. And by the way—hint, hint—when the tide is out the fishing isn't great. My advice is: just leave the breed with the show people. Let them add it to their growing collection of unusual dogs.

LOG DOGS

Another type of already-bailedale is the log dog. These floaters are a remarkable example of the evolutionary principle of convergence: coming from a completely different ancestral strain (the punting dogs), log dogs now perform a similar task for the fisherman as the floating mat dogs do.

Log dogs were developed by a few smart hunters (they are too few to list their names here). They are therefore an illustration of the evolutionary principle of taking something good and making it much more useful; for example, taking a hunting dog and making it into a fishing dog. The first log dogs were short-legged Chesapeake Bay retrievers (market hunting dogs). This local variety was developed in the early 1800s in the upper bay area, where punt gunners bred and trained their dogs to swim alongside their boats and not get in and out all the time.

Now, many of us have trouble imagining just what the nineteenth century was like. Foraging for wild game was much more important then, simply because the supermarket had not been invented yet. Wild things cluttered the landscape, darkened the sun, and clogged the rivers. People tried to solve this problem by eating them all, but they had to double their own population in order to accomplish this task. Hunters specialized in eliminating certain kinds of wildlife; the commercial punt gunners were really challenged by the terrific numbers of ducks and waterfowl which lived in or migrated through the Chesapeake Bay.

Hunters were good in the nineteenth century. They could get all the game and sometimes, as in the case of the passenger pigeon, they did. Dogs were better, too. Today, bird-dog owners brag that their dog can do "doubles," and if Curly can do triples he gets written up in a national magazine. But in the nineteenth century a dog might bring in three hundred ducks a day for a punt gunner. That's about one duck every two-and-a-half minutes.

Now imagine a typical punt hunter's day. At around half past five in the afternoon, he shoots the 280th duck. He has to "mark" each bird for the dog, like we do today: "Meat [dog's name], ober dhare Meat," he says, pointing to the 280th duck of the day. Mercy. The guy would be popping throat lozenges like a drug addict and he'd have punt gunner's finger, worn out from pointing. If Meat was anything like my son's Chessies, the guy would also have a frozen finger, because the dog has to see the actual finger in order to get the correct general direction. There is no hiding the finger in a glove for these highly trained, intelligent dogs. They need to see the real finger.

For the 280th time, Meat leaps out of the boat,[5] giving it a little thrust backward as he accelerates forward. By now,

---

5 Again, if Meat is anything like my son's dogs, he would be very discerning about where he jumps over the side of the boat. Tigger's Chessies run around at the gunwales for about ten minutes looking for the exact right spot. We had to switch to padded fiberglass boats because the ticky-tucky of their little nails on the aluminum made an unpleasant sound on a wet, raw duck-hunting day. Often we wore ear muffs even on warm and delightful days.

in fact, the poor guy would be off the coast of North Carolina, and have a serious case of whiplash.

Also, each time Meat leaps out of the boat, he has to swim farther and farther to the ducks because the boat would be getting farther and farther away.

And each time Meat gets back to the boat, he clambers in. If I may extrapolate from my son's dogs, I'd guess Meat could turn that boat's sides to hamburger in just a few entrées.

Have you ever seen a dog clamber into a boat? It's just too incredible. My son's old Chessie, Scoter, had to be the all-time champion at clambering. Placing her forefeet on the gunwale, she would begin a series of cranking motions with her left hind foot. Against the side of an aluminum boat it sounded melodic and eerie, increasing in tempo until it brought to mind the Andrews Sisters singing eight to the bar.[6]

Each rotation of the leg and foot would gain her a millimeter in the up-and-in direction. The leg would now be going at the speed of light, but, unlike the arm of an old record player that follows the groove, this armature creates its own grooves in the side of the boat.

Faster and faster, the leg dug for bauxite. After several minutes she would get her head over the gunwale. The second movement involved a tympanic percussion solo as she

---

6 We keep Scoter in shape in the off season by turning her on her back and scratching that magic spot on her tummy, triggering the phantom-scratching reflex. First one side, then the other. A couple of isometric minutes a day is all that's needed to keep her ready for the boat.

positioned her head under the seat. Initially this "head tuck under seat" motion would be accomplished with a harmonized drumming of the top of her head on the bottom of the seat. Then came the Anne Boleyn movement: with her head ... tucked ... underneath the seat ... she walked ... her head along ... leveraging with her neck and bringing her body up horizontal to the plane of the water.

Once Scoter got her head firmly lodged under the seat, both hind feet could work in harmony, though she often jazzed it up with syncopation. The final movement started with an arpeggio of elbow, which breached the gunwale.[7]

With a final drumming roll the dog was in. A lot of sea water came in, too. This drained immediately into the bilge where it began to separate into layers. The heavy water sank to the bottom while the finer grades of Chesapeake oils sat delicately on top. In the early stages of separation one got quite colorful little rainbow effects.

But Scoter is a direct descendant of the bilgies (yes, Chessies have that distinction[8]), and duty called her. There was water in the boat, which instinct demanded she must expel. She must, inevitably, monsoon. She often stood, not

7 The gunwale ("gun wall") is the top side of the boat where the cannon was installed; it was not only instrumental in letting the cannonball out, but to this day it remains important for not letting the water in.

8 Chesapeake Bay retrievers were bilge pups as late as the nineteenth century; there is evidence that a pair of Chesapeake ancestors were washed out from the bilge of a shipwreck off the coast of Maryland in 1807.

in the fore-and-aft-the-beam position, but rather in the strad-
dle-the-thwart position, while monsooning. Now the rainbows were really gorgeous. She is not a lazy dog and would
continue this health-giving behavior until all the water was
gone, no matter how long it took. I say health-giving
because my cigar often went out with the first monsoon,
and was usually unrelightable.

I'm not quite sure what happened next because I regu-
larly used the intermission to clean my glasses. But I think
this was when she presented the bouquet of duck to Tigger.
The performance over, we'd get busy again, cleaning the
salt spray off our guns so they wouldn't pit, and making the
usual duct tape repairs on the seat cushions. Now came the
part of the performance that I lived for.

Tigger would raise his frozen finger toward the open
sea, and say, "Fetch." Yes, Scoter could do doubles. But she
always, after numerous circumlocutions, left the boat from
the same spot. I don't know if it was just instinct, or whether
Tigger taught her this way. Whatever, she usually forgot
where that special place was, and she searched rapidly for it,
disturbing the little layerings of water, which again put out
little rainbows of protest as they figured out their layer pat-
terning once more.

Tigger and I can't afford to shoot more than a couple of
ducks a season. The cost of boats has gone up since the days
of Meat and the punt gunners (everything has gone up,
except the number of ducks), and a good dog can wear out

an average boat even in a poor season of shooting. Mostly, I go to be with my boy and his dog, and don't shoot anything—it's just part of my conservation ethic (of boats, that is).

It will be pretty obvious to the reader that the early punt gunner couldn't have Meat get in and out of the boat three hundred times a day. Based on our experience with Scoter, in three hundred retrieves Meat could wear out sixty-five boats a day.

No. The dog had to stay in the water, out with the decoys if possible. If it could learn to anticipate the shooting and be there, the dog only had to swim one way (back to the boat) after the duck was shot.

At its most effective, this in-water retriever had a head that stuck out of the water (this is important for several reasons), and it (the head) looked like a duck. Some dogs, mostly Chesapeake Bay retrievers, had really ducky heads and floated low in the water with only their head showing. This resulted in an almost-perfect duck mimic, so they could be used as decoys as well as retrievers. Properly trained, such dogs were actually better than wooden decoys: their moving around, sniffing noses, and generally taking an interest in each other made for realistic, ducky behavior.

Now, some of the more observant punt gunners noticed that fish were collecting under the dog on bright days. After all, these dogs were bred for short legs and webbed toes, so they wouldn't even contemplate climbing into a boat. They were round and log-shaped, with plenty of body fat, so they would float better.

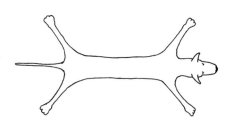

LOG DOG (PLAN VIEW)

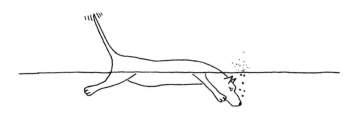

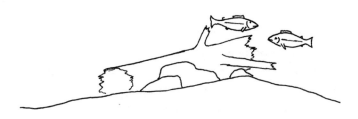

LOG DOG (SIDE VIEW)

Many a punt gunner, under duckless skies, would fish a dog. The smarter ones began to realize that as duck populations dwindled they could supplement their incomes with fish, and they began to breed those dogs that attracted fish. The curly retriever coat remained tight against the dog even when wet, and looked very much like tree bark. (Not to be confused with tree barking, another phenomenon perfected by hunters in their dogs.) The best ones even smelled like fish, a trait that also has been passed along to our present-day retrievers.

Thus the log dogs germinated. When punt gunning as a commercial venture was outlawed, duck-headed dogs still had value in their shadows, and so they were still bred—but now they were bred for fishing. At first, it required great skill by the fishermen to get these dogs to look and behave like a log and not a duck. But over the years, log dogs have evolved nicely from animal quackers to cheerie oaks.

Because of these dogs' stubby legs, pudgy bodies, duck-like heads, and fishy smell, some thought the log dogs were in fact basset hounds. Given the enunciation of fishermen, this was soon corrupted to bassin hound, a breed name by which log dogs are commonly known. Following the widespread acceptance of this name, a reformation of the mythologies and assumptions shrouding the breed led to the dogma that they were bred intentionally for largemouth fishermen. This is now true, but it was not so originally.

Bassin hounds are a distinct variety of gillie dogs and are headed for breed status. Shadiness is their cardinal virtue, but unlike the other raft breeds (for example, floating mat dogs), bassins always take an active interest in finding fish. They float slowly toward a fish and, when it is underneath them, they blow easily out of their nostrils, making little bubbles[9] that rise to the surface and signal the alert fisherman where to cast.

Fishing Your Log Dog

Fishers of largemouth bass set their dogs in the shallows along banks, arranged in realistic fashion. Once the dog is in position, it should take an active interest in the mimicry. If the dog can sink just slightly at the tail end, it achieves the half submerged, waterlogged look that is highly desirable in some locations. I have never seen the variety that sinks at the head end.

A conscientious logdogger constantly checks on his dogs. In reservoirs with rising and falling water, the dog's position has to be constantly monitored. Many a fisherman who has set up ten or more log dogs has lost one because it drifted, unnoticed, off the bank and ended up at some paper mill. The fact that your dog could end up as the front page of *The*

---

9 Environmentalists long thought these were methane bubbles. Even though bassins do emit pure methane from one end, this can be strictly controlled through diet. No conscientious fisherman would add to global warming by feeding his dog improperly.

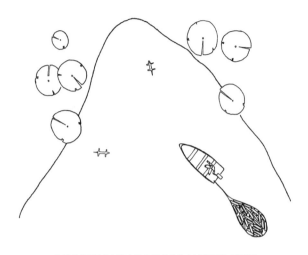

ROUNDING UP LOG DOGS (AERIAL VIEW)

New York Times should be enough to make you pay attention. A map takes time to make but it is well worth it in the end. Attention to detail can save the angler many hours slogging through rafts of logs looking for his favorite working dog. Some of the best log mimics have been retrieved by campers and, unfortunately, used for roasting marshmallows. Down south, alligators can be a problem and the fisherman can end up with a bunch of petrified dogs.

Choosing A Log Dog

Fly-fishing logdoggers tend to give their dogs names like Driftwood, Sandalwood, or Lincoln. You see their registration forms inscribed with the likes of "Champion Dreadknot of Basswood." Girllies (another kind of sportsman's helper) usually call their log dogs Twiggy, Splinters, or Yule. Of course, coarse fishermen like my friend Stan call theirs Bark, Pulp, or Punky. Such a dog, registered with the AKC, might be G.D. Snag, referring to its grand dam status, so G.C.D. before a dog's name would refer to the Grand Coulee Dam, a famous river obstruction up in Washington State. There is a knack to selecting log puppies. Don't pick the runt, no matter how cute it is: always keep that old song in mind and be sure you gitta long little doggie. (Humming it is helpful during the selection process to keep you focused on log scales.) Remember where you are going to fish the dog and try to match the local timber. For instance, pitch-stained patterns on knotty pine backgrounds are popular in the northwestern states.

Stan and I had a great log dog once. Butt always looked like he was on the way to the pulp mill. He became totally immersed in his role as a log. He was truly one with the environment. He looked so waterlogged that he got the Deep Ecology Award in 1985. I loved to sit and watch him in the morning. Turtles crawled up on his back to sun themselves, waiting for their breakfast, while I waited for mine. If fish didn't come around, Butt drifted slowly over to them.

STRINGER SPANIELS

Fishing dogs like Butt started out as one thing which they weren't so good at and became another. This illustrates the difference between fishing and hunting dogs: fishing dogs became useful and quietly go about their work, so you don't ever hear of them; hunting dogs, most of which have had to be signed up for preservation by the AKC, usually only perfect their barking parts.

This difference illustrates the difference between hunters and fishers. One should not put any value judgment on these differences (which is the nature of prejudice, after all); in an objective book such as this, one simply records the differences and lets it go at that. Of course, sometimes one might just delicately point out the differences and offer them up as constructive criticism. What I'm trying to say here, in a nice way, is that hunters use dogs in some ways that are just plain stupid and take the joy out of the sport.

The biggest difference (probably to be legalistic about it I should say, "in my opinion"), the biggest and dumbest difference between modern hunters-with-dogs and fishers-with-dogs, in my opinion, is: hunters are the kind of people whose dog finds the game; the dog is the one that retrieves it, and the hunter person is the one who carries the game home. The fisher person, on the other hand, has the thrill of finding the fish and providing the expertise for capturing the fish, and his dog carries the fish home. This, naturally, is what stringer spaniels are for.

In early times, before this breed arose, hunters and fishers both carried their trophies home, and they had the same basic techniques. Hunters clung religiously to these traditions. At first, they tied a string around the game and carried it over the shoulder. This system was pretty good, except that other hunters, seeing game going through the forest in this position, were never quite sure if the game was afoot or if it was dead. Often they would shoot it again to make sure. This led to the development of the pocket. After a hunter shot a pheasant, for example, he would put it in the large pocket in the back of his coat. Then other hunters could tell whether the pheasant was dead or not by smelling the pocket. You could smell the pocket up to several years later if you were curious whether the pheasant was still dead. Getting deer into a pocket is more of a problem and hunters still drag a deer around, letting other hunters shoot it over and over until all concur that it is dead.

Fishermen have their equivalents: stringers (more on these below), vests with pockets, and cute little baskets called creels. These wicker hampers have a little teeny hole in the top so fly-fishermen can slip their fish in without even opening the cover. Creels have become standard equipment for fly-fishermen, part of the uniform, so to speak, and even catch and release fishermen like Will Ryan (FSW) are still required to carry one.

Now, Stan carries a stringer most of the time. A stringer is basically a length of "unbreakable" line which the successful fisher threads between the fish's gills and through its mouth. He then is supposed to tie the two ends to the boat and lower the strung fish into the water. Stringers come in many designs, from the very simple and easy to use to the much more difficult and nearly impossible to use. This latter is a chain with huge side-branching safety pins. Stan seems to require one thing of his stringers: they must sink if you drop one over the side. Furthermore, they must be so heavy that they will convey all the fish to the deepest part of the pond. His stringers provide us with hours of fun playing grapple. Stanley eventually came up with the idea of a stringer spaniel. As usual, if I found the dog and trained the dog he'd pay half and I could keep it at my place.

Stringer spaniels have curly coats, about the consistency of Velcro tape. In fact, using one of these dogs is very much like using Velcro tape. The fact that fish are scaly and have gill covers and gill arches and gill rakes means it is really easy to stick one to the dog. Just take the fish by its tail and middle and shove the head into the dog's fur. Any place will do, as long as there is not already a fish there. For some people this is not a problem. I like to balance my fish across the dog. Regardless, nothing gives me more satisfaction than watching a stringer come home at night, loaded.

The Origin of the Stringer Spaniel

Many famous breeds have obscure origins.[10] The stringer spaniel is no exception. I'd always assumed that the stringer was a derivative of the log dogs. Log dogs hang around in

---

10 Most of these now-famous but once-obscure dogs are hunting dogs. I think this is because hunters don't realize what they have if it is working OK. It is only when the dog is no good and they have to get it registered that they look for its origins.

STRINGER SPANIEL

the water and have those bark-mimicking coats. It seems to me it would be easy for evolution to make the little leap to a full-blown stringer. But, I must admit, I really don't know where they came from or who made the connection that you could stick a fish to a dog.

I asked Stanley one time where he first heard about them. He immediately went into mumble mode and said something like, he hadn't heard about them and thought I'd made a mistake, and he had really said, "springer spaniel." That didn't make any sense to me because Stanley couldn't stick a fish to a springer even with potato glue.

As it turned out, I didn't have any trouble finding one. I just put out the word and this guy called one night and said that his brother raises them in Yugoslavia. So, even though they were expensive I ordered a breeding pair. I've always been partial to imported dogs.

Choosing and Using Your Stringer Spaniel

Stringers come in all sizes, and you should get a size that suits your typical fishing experience. If you are like me, get a very large stringer spaniel. If you are like Stan, you should get a dog with a steel wool tongue for polishing the utensils, and chisel-sharp front teeth for getting the home fries off the pan. If you are like Will Ryan (FSW) and don't like bringing a lot of fish home,[11] then a toy stringer is good enough. I always think it's cute when you open up Will's basket and there is a creel stringer. The little tyke sticks her head out of the tiny hole in the top and watches the old FSW flipping the poly horsehair. When we go off as a group, Will's dog is always a second stringer.

Stringers can be tethered to the side of the boat during the day and fish can be added to them right in the water. This keeps both the fish and dog fresh so they don't start smelling. In small ponds I don't even tie my dog. When we

---

11 People who like to catch and release or practice other forms of not bringing fish home can stop reading this section and go directly to the chapter on spotter dogs (page 73). Spotter dogs can help you find the fish to catch so that you might actually need a stringer spaniel in the future.

move the boat to a new set of lily pads, the dog follows by himself later on. It's more interesting for the dog if it is allowed to explore on its own. But it should know to hustle right over when someone yells, "Fish on!" Unless that someone is a fly fisherman like Will (FSW), who gives the fish a sporting chance for an hour or so. Then there is no particular hurry.

If you work your dog with the free float technique, you should try to put the same number and size of fish on each side of the dog. Don't, for instance, put all the big ones on one side. Since the fish are still alive, they continue to swim even though they are stuck to the dog, and they can exert considerable vector forces that interfere with his unidirectional swimming: having all the big fish on one side may require the dog to swim in one great big circle in order to get to you. In an extreme case, the dog might just pivot *in situ*.

A fatal "fault" in some stringers is the rolling gene, widely exhibited by not-so-well-bred stringer spaniels. This behavior, shared with many non-stringer breeds, was unfortunately ignored by some irresponsible breeders. One breeder actually selected for this behavior, trying to turn it into a virtue, by claiming that the dog is loading its own fish. Like many bad genes, the fish rolling behavior has swept through the dog world like a bona fide genetic disease. Just let my son Tigger's dog outside and she'll travel miles to find dead fish and pick them up by Velcroing. She is usually successful unless she meets a porcupine first. Dogs instinctively know that dead fish should be Velcroed to them: right behind their ears and on their shoulders where your hand goes when you stroke them. This fish rolling sometimes gets so bad that several once-fine working breeds have actually been registered.

Stan always teaches his dogs to roll over on command, something that puzzles me. "What on earth do you have in mind?" I query. "What practical value could rolling on command have for a dog?" Stan mumbles something about if the dog should burst into flame and you are not able to find a heavy blanket. After our first stringer, Threads, mushed 250 fish into perch purée, I think Stan learned his lesson about rolling on command.

Fish Spotter Dogs

LIKE THE GILLIES, THE FISH SPOTTERS ARE ONE OF THE TWO main classifications of fishing dogs. While some of the gillies (notably the bassin hound and the more intelligent floating mat dogs) have some spotting abilities, fish spotters are specifically named for their acute looking skills. Fishermen think they are named for their marking abilities, as the name "spotter" implies. This is confusing to many non–dog-experts and hunters, and to AKC representatives who give talks at annual meetings. Let me try to clear up this confusion between sporting dogs and spotting dogs.

Often, in the field, a hunter will say "mark" to his pointer, when the dog looks in a meaningful way at, say (usually), a bird. To "mark" in human-to-dog sense is to use the nose to look. In this case, the dog's nose directs the human's eyes. If the dog smells a bird, the human looks in the direction of the smell until he comes upon the bird. At that point, he yells "mark," and the dog tries to claim the bird. But the bird flies up and the hunter has to shoot it so the dog can reclaim and eat it, which is why it wanted to claim it in the first place. The dog interprets the command "mark" in the "claim as mine" category of behavior.[1]

---

1 One of the best Chessie trainers I know is named Mark; his dog named him.

Contrast this behavior with what wolves do. Like dogs, wolves chase deer, but unlike dogs, they do not mark birds. Wolves mark territories ("this area is mine"). Now, to train a bird dog to mark a bird the same way a wolf claims his territory goes against everybody's best instincts. Wolves claim territories by marking the boundaries with a secret message system. When wolves turned into dogs they kept the same code books, but since dogs have moved into the suburbs where there are fewer trees, they mark telephone poles, fire hydrants, and coffee tables to signal the edges of their territory. Since there are fewer of these scent posts in the suburbs than there were trees in the forest, more messages have to be left on each one.

A pointer marks birds with its nose. Therein the similarity between wolves and dogs breaks down, because wolves are smelling where they have been marking. But if dogs marked birds as territorial boundaries, then what? Thus, bird dogs are totally confused when they point a bird and the hunters say "mark," and so the dogs usually revert to chasing deer.

When hunters say "mark" what they really mean is "jump." "Jump, dog, where you are smelling." If wolves jumped where they were smelling they'd kill themselves. All the breeds of hunting dogs have figured out the differences except the red setters which continue to jump into trees.

The fish spotter dogs aren't like the coffee-table markers. They don't mark by making a spot: they spot by looking.

They look at the fish. The fisherman looks where the dog is looking and there is a fish. Spotters don't smell. Regardless of what anybody tells you, dogs can't smell underwater. They smell everyplace else, but not underwater.

Spotters are fish finders, and they come in several categories: pike pointers, angler dogs, tippups, and rocky pointers. All are magnificent, intelligent companions and another example of superior selective breeding.

My favorite fish spotter breed is the rocky pointer, which is probably the best of the pike pointers. I started using them because electronic fish finders have been a constant problem for me. It's frustrating to work one if your fishing buddy is Stan.

Fishing is one of those times when two guys can go out in a boat and quietly do their thing. There is no need to talk. The best fishing buddies (Stan is mine) can go for days without saying a word. But with one of those electronic fish finders in the boat, the peace of the wilderness, the stealth of the stalk, is shattered. "How deep is it now?" "Is it still three feet?" "See anything on the scope?" "How deep is it now?" "Move back to three feet!"

I finally had to get Stan his own depth finder. Other fishermen probably wonder why my modest fourteen-foot aluminum boat has two fairly serious depth finders in it. The reasoning was Stan could look at his own depth finder and all would be quiet again. But it was not to be. "What does your depth finder say?" "Huh; mine says two-and-a-half feet."

It was another one of those cases where we had to get another dog.

PIKE POINTERS

It is exciting seeing a pike pointer at work: he stands in the boat, sticking his head over the side and underwater. When his tail stiffens and starts to vibrate, and his front leg draws up against his chest in a point, you know right where the keeper fish is! Well, you almost know where it is.

With pike pointers, there is a problem the average pheasant hunter doesn't have. With upland field dogs you know exactly where the bird is by projecting an imaginary line from between the dog's eyes, bisecting the nostrils and on down the smell line out to meet the ground—where, sometimes, there is a bird. Good dogs look where they are pointing while bad dogs point where they are looking. Most hunters don't seem to be able to tell the difference.

But because of physical principles that govern ground, light, and water, pike pointers are not looking where you think they are looking. Unless you are jigging for flounders, fish are not usually on the ground, but rather suspended between the ground (underwater, the technical term is "bottom") and the surface of the water.

Here is the main point. Underwater, the imaginary line is even more imaginary than if it were out of water. Therefore, you have to make some calculations, based on the dog's point of view, to determine the real depth and direction of the fish. Using the imaginary line ploy, you need to know the distance along imaginary line A (see figure I) to the fish. When your imaginary line gets to the fish, project it straight up so that it intersects the surface at right angles (imaginary line B). The length of imaginary line B is equivalent to the depth of the fish.

You now know how deep to run your lure.

This book is not written for beginners, but if you are a beginner, realize that most manufacturers publish the depth at which the lure runs right on the package, and if you are a clever person your package is in your lure box. This is the manufacturer's response to deep ecology: it not only helps you run at the proper depth but it keeps you from littering.

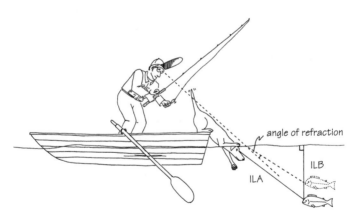

FIGURE I: PIKE POINTER TRIGONOMETRY

Although you now know how deep to run the lure, believe it or not, you don't know where the fish is. That is because when you drew imaginary line B straight from the fish to the surface, you assumed that if you went straight back down B you would find the fish. But you are wrong. The fish at the end of the imaginary line was an imaginary fish. The real fish is a few feet away.

You need to calculate the real, as distinct from the perceived, direction.[2]

The dog has his head underwater and is looking directly at the fish. You can't see the fish. If you could you wouldn't need the dog. The dog is looking at a different place than you are, even though you are both trying to look at the same place, the fish. Your projected imaginary line from the dog's eyes across its nose on out into the depths is not a real imaginary line, but an imaginary imaginary line. You have to calculate the difference between the imaginary line you are imagining and the imaginary line you should be imagining.

Example: The dog's imaginary line (from now on called IL) is exactly at right angles to the surface. This means that the fish is under the boat. You should use some kind of jig. Simple enough, but there is a complication that has to be accounted for in all other calculations other than the perpendicular illustration.

---

2 Many of my students have to reread this section several times so don't feel bad if you don't quite get it the first time.

Normally, the pike pointer's point will be correct, that is, his IL is accurate, but his head is underwater and yours shouldn't be. This means you have to calculate the angle of refraction. Surface refraction or the bending of the light happens when light goes from an aqueous medium to a gaseous medium, for example, from the water to the air above it.

It helps to know some geometry, trigonometry, and if the boat is moving, calculus. The formula is based on the angle that your head is displaced from the obtuse angle the dog is pointing. If you are standing right over the dog then this is no problem because your IL is theoretically in the same direction as the dog's, except yours is running along the surface and his is underwater. That means you can't calculate the depth of the fish. That, in conjunction with refraction, also means your IL is longer than his IL, even though the actual distance is the same for both of you. This is one of those cases where you do not question your dog: the dog knows best.

To say this is no problem is a slight misstatement. If you are standing right over the dog and the dog has its head underwater, leaning over the side of the boat, that means you and the dog are on the same side of the boat and therefore both your heads are over the same side of the boat: you may experience the capsizing boat syndrome. There are two solutions to this problem: 1) get a gyro dog as big as you and the pointer combined, or 2) learn how to compute the refraction angles. Please look at figure I for an example of a refraction angle.

To return to the depth problem, which some of you mathematicians probably thought I was avoiding, when you have the true IL calculated, you have to compute the distance to the fish, because you need to know not only how deep the fish is, but how far it is, since in most cases you can't see it. Both distances are easier to determine than the refraction angles, because they can't be computed mathematically; but both can be estimated. If the initial angle is small and the bottom is shallow then accuracy is not very important. It is when the bottom is sixty feet away and the fish are suspended at ten feet that we have a problem.

But from watching these dogs I learned a little trick. A pike pointer positions its tail directly over its back and wags it in figure eights.[3] The speed of the tail wag is an approximation of how far the fish is from the dog's nose. You must remember that there is an inverse correlation between the rate of tail movement and the length of the IL. Fast moving tails mean short ILs, but slow moving tails may only mean anticipation of a fish that has not appeared yet. With a little practice you'll become an expert at interpreting the dog's signals.

To gauge the distance more accurately, check which part of the tail is wagging. If it's just the tip, the fish is very

---

3 People are always wondering what dogs mean by wagging their tails. The answer is, "How long is it until supper?"

close; the whole tail wagging from the base means the fish is far away. How far? Well, I find that the point of wag corresponds to the length of the IL. In other words, if a dog is wagging halfway down the tail, then the fish is halfway down the Potential Imaginary Line (PIL), which is the distance the dog can see underwater.

The PIL varies with water conditions. At the beginning of the fishing day, stick your head underwater and have your fishing buddy pull out a measuring tape. When you can't see his hand any more, record the distance: this is your base PIL. Remember that a dog can see slightly farther than a human, and of course changes in cloud cover and water turbulence will change the PIL hourly.

Dozing when the dog is working, or not making the calculations speedily, is unfair to the dog. Pike pointers that get stuck on point need attention much more quickly than does an English pointer that can't shake a bobwhite. Natural selection has operated much more quickly on pike pointers than on English pointers, which is why the former have never required registration with your local kennel club.

Training Your Pike Pointer

Training a pike pointer is no more difficult than training the average red setter. All the standard equipment is used: the fish-shaped bumpers, the release traps, the whistle, the two-by-four. I use a twenty-four-foot davit, so I can lower a fish in the trap in full view.

Begin by training the dog to point at the fish above water; then as you gradually lower the fish into the water, the dog follows it down. Not too gradually, however, because don't forget the fish has got breathing troubles in the above-water phase of the training, just as the dog does in the below-water phase. Stan likes to use an aquarium to help with training. But that's not for me. Somehow sitting in the middle of a pond with an aquarium dangling from a twenty-four-foot boom while saying "good dog good dog good dog" at the pike pup feels kind of silly, especially because most of the other guys on the pond never heard of rocky pointers and I can just imagine what they are saying to each other. Besides, I don't think this method is very effective, and it's not good for the dog. Stan can't use a very big aquarium unless we put an outrigger on the boat, so he trains the dog on little fish. But then the dog learns to point little fish, which adds to Stan's fishing problems. I never go with Stan when he is training his dog. I tell him I have to mow the lawn or do windows. He seems to understand.

Stan starts the dog at home pointing fish in the aquarium. When the dog can't keep his eyes off the fish tank then Stan hangs it off the back porch with some monofilament. When the dog seems to have that down pat, Stan slowly lowers the aquarium into his swimming pool. Every time he lets the dog out, the dog sees the fish line going into the pool and, thinking that his favorite aquarium is at the end, he (the dog) sticks his head underwater. Finally Stan just keeps the monofilament in the pool and the dog keeps sticking his head in the pool looking for the aquarium.

Eventually, we blindfold the dog for the car ride, and keep the blindfold on until we get to the middle of the lake. Then we just dangle a line over the side of the boat. When the blindfold is removed the dog sees the line, thinks there is a box with a fish in it under the water, and begins to look for it. You've won. "Good boy, clever fellow, well done."

Pike pointers and rocky pointers usually are given regal names like their terrestrial counterparts. English pointers always seem to have baronial names that never quite sit right for me. Champion Bowling Feet of Maple Alley should have a robe and a crown and maybe a scepter, but to me English pointers always look naked. I'd reflect that naked-ness in the name, for example, Alley's Oops, or Alley By By.

I believe dog names should follow a theme—a theme that says something about the dog and its behavior. Perhaps I'd combine this with giving them names that speak of our American Indian traditions. How about, Chiefly Stuck-on-Point? Thematic variations might include: Brave Can't-Find-the-Bird, or, Eat-the-Bird. Once you know the breed well the possibilities are endless.

The tradition carries over into the pike pointers but in a different way. The aqueous environments they work in should be respected. Samples for the rocky pointers are: Two-Darn-Cold, Two-Fish, or Take-A-Breath. Some people use these dogs strictly in salt water applications and name the dogs accordingly, for example, Rusty.

ANGLER DOGS

Angler dogs are descended from do-it-yourself pike pointers although they look more like the pikes than the pointers. They resemble nothing so much as the angler fish. An angler fish is an ugly critter with a big mouth, with lots of teeth and something like a rubber worm dangling from the roof of the mouth. This worm mimic is a loose hanging organ that looks like the top of your mouth feels after you bite into a right-out-of-the-oven pizza. The angler fish sits with its mouth hanging open, waving the pizza flap. The first anchovy that nibbles the dangle gets a final lesson in stimulus and response. The mouth, containing a jillion teeth, snaps shut. There is no such thing as a have-a-heart angler fish. Neither are there catch and release angler fish.

Angler dogs don't have the pizza flap, but rather a modified (some might say deformed) tongue. The tongue looks like an Arkansas crawler (an earthworm): it is shaped like a thick brown corkscrew. In its relaxed position, it hangs out of the dog's mouth, and it can also be withdrawn into the dog's mouth in a series of little jerks, giving it a lifelike motion that is attractive to fish.

The lifelike jerks are a result of the panting muscles. Normal dog tongues go in and out when a dog pants; this facilitates the action of the saliva groove (*cavia linguini*) which runs down the center of the tongue. Angler dogs don't have this trenched tongue, and they can only pant underwater (more on that in a minute).

Angler Dog Appearance and Standard

Angler dogs are serious dogs, and not for everybody. Their faces are piranha-like, with uncountable needle-like teeth. Often there are teeth where you wouldn't expect dogs to have teeth. The teeth in the upper jaw are skewed slightly from those in the lower jaw: this is a major plus in the breed. If their teeth lined up perfectly, they would slice the fish in half, the way a bird dog sometimes crush-bites a bird.

The best angler dog tongue color is earthworm (naturally). The second best color (though more rare) is white. Glow white is especially great for night fishing for bullheads. Considerable variation in color is allowed for show dogs. As usual some of the show breeders have missed the point of why angler dogs are important. Last year a guy took best of breed with a dog that had a camouflage colored tongue.

The tongue should be not only colored like an earthworm, but shaped like an earthworm. It should be long and narrow, with a clearly segmented appearance. Lateral constrictions producing clearly demarcated segments are acceptable. The tongue must never be normal. A Scruffs judge once disqualified a dog with an earthworm tattoo on a normal tongue.

The nose of the angler dog is an exaggerated bulldog shape. The original bulldogs had nostrils pointing dorsally, allowing the dog to breathe while its snout was buried in the deep warm folds of the bull's neck. The angler dog is similarly designed, but the nostrils are more pronounced and farther back on its snout. The nostrils have migrated with the rostrum, to a position almost between the eyes. Here is a dog that smells exactly the way it looks.

All breeds of dogs have a twitch or sniff muscle around the nostrils. This allows them to sample air in little pulses, increasing the concentrations of smells. These constrictoid muscles also prevent entry of flies, which are curious as to why dogs smell that way. In the angler dog the dorsally-situated nostrio-constrictoid muscles are modified into a cartilaginous flap, which stops water from flowing into the dog's head if the nostroids descend below the aqueous plane. Otherwise, because of its unique conformation, the dog would have water on the brain.

Like beagles (see page 11), angler dogs come in different sizes. For general purposes, the popular #2 Victor with padded jaws is best, though bear trap models with multiple serrations are also available. Stan likes the .5 Oneida for miniature baleen anglers, while I tend to like the 10x sizes. Then again he prefers quality perchy pan size fish. Stan finds cleaning small fish a challenge, so he catches a lot of them.

Angler Dog Physiology, with a Digression on Drool

As I have hinted, the driving principle of a good angler dog is temperature control. Just about everybody knows that normal dogs cool themselves with a series of pants. Pants come in pairs, the in- and ex-haling, also known as sucking and blowing, or drawing and pushing, air over the moistened tongue. It is mostly the exudate that we are concerned with here. (I'll save the inudate for the advanced course.)

Dog exudate is a gaseous vapor that is specially adapted to take heat and highly toxic chemicals away from the dog. You know immediately when the dog is in the toxic chemical phase of the cycle, but heat transfer is undetectable unless the dog is on fire (see rolling, page 71). The exudate transfers heat from the tongue to the surroundings. This process causes a deterioration of the molasses-like salivary formula, which the dog fortifies by eating grass and rolling in fish (again, see page 71). The salivary formula can be adjusted to essence of skunk oil, which you doggy people know is popular with most of our domestic breeds. Tincture of Abyssinian civet is a favorite of my dogs, while my son Tigger's dogs specialize in northern pike paste.

Dog saliva is unique in other ways. Production is in a pair of organs, the *grandulosus salivalarium* complex. God only knows why they are paired. In most domestic dogs these two organs make twice as much cooling fluids as necessary, to store in case of emergencies: for instance, when a hot spell is unforecasted and the dog is caught in, rather than under, the house. Each *grandulosus* duct has a bivalve, which operates with clam-like precision to release the excess exudate continuously into the environment. The *grandulosus salivalarium* has nonstick walls to prevent salivary molasses from sludging before it reaches the outside of the dog.

The *cavia linguini*, or saliva groove, trenches the medial portion of the tongue from the *grandulosus salivalarium* to the anterior edges (trench tongue). Its particular function is to mold the salivary molasses into long strings. Once a string has absorbed sufficient heat, the dog can release it (the heat infested portions) in a gesture similar to that of an Argentinean *vaquero* catching an ostrich with a bola.

The technical term for the whole process is evapio-drooling (named for the Italian physiologist Lumbardo Evapio, 1870–1933). Evapio-drooling is the most common method of preventing boil-over in dogs. When dogs are thermally stressed they place the cooling molasses on other portions of their bodies that feel hot. With small head shakes, they can reposition the entire contents of the *salivalarium* to the surface of their face, thus increasing the surface area where evapio-cooling takes place. Hot dogs also redirect the flow of cooling fluid to their front paws and legs. Some dogs, such as Saint Bernards, can make a small muddy pond, or dog-walla, in which they lie.

My son Tigger's Chessies have perfected these techniques. Their evolutionary advancement is the combining of evapio-drooling with instinctive monsooning. This allows them to place the cooling drool on ceilings and walls, where it acts as organic air-conditioning: an adaptive breakthrough allows them to cool their environment rather than their body. Dogs could give us the solution to global warming.

As you can see, the key factor for hot dogs is surface area. In order for dogs to evapio-cool properly they have to have gigantic tongues. I've seen dogs with tongues half the length of their bodies with great huge medial trenches full to the brim with refrigeration fluids. These dogs could practically freeze to death on a hot day.

The miracle of the angler dog lies in its small convoluted tongue with the surface area of an earthworm. No *grandulosus salivalarium*, no *cavia linguini*, no cooling molasses. The angler dog does not have enough tongue area for evapio-drooling to effect evapio-cooling. This condition is exacerbated in larger angler dogs: small dogs' tongues are the size of actual earthworms. But so are those of the large dogs. No matter what you do to a dog, you can't change the size of an earthworm.

Angler dogs solve the cooling problem by soaking their tongues in water. Water cools the tongue much faster than air, so keeping its tongue submerged in water allows the dog to pump hot blood through the earthworm at a more leisurely pace.

I love my anglers. When I come home at night they don't even look up from their water dishes—they can't, for fear their tongues will come out of the water. They roll their eyes in my direction and I know they are happy to see me. They are not the kind of dog that jumps all over you, hosing down your suit with cooling molasses and drooly paws, like some Chessies. I have never been slimed by an angler dog.

As I go to hang up my coat they do these funny little hops around the dish so they can continue to see me. Of course I know what they want. But in ritualistic fashion I go about my business just as if I've forgotten all about treat time. They shuffle around their bowls again and watch me look at the mail. Then all of a sudden I look up as if I just noticed them for the first time. Their stubby tails begin to wag. "Oh," I say, "Daddy's little fish dogs want their treat." The tail waggle is alarming now and I hustle to the refrigerator to bring the episode to a conclusion before their tongues come out of water with all the excitement. They look happy as I bring the treats over, but the only noise you hear is their stubby tails thumping on the floor as I slip fresh ice cubes into their dishes.

ANGLER DOG, COOLING

Here are a couple of tips about angler dogs around the house. If all the water evaporates from their dish the dogs will begin to migrate: as a precaution I keep the bathroom door shut at all times. They can't bark while tongue-soaking, so smoke and burglar alarms should be well maintained. Finally, hiccups are more serious in this breed than in others: one good hiccup can siphon a bowl dry.

Fishing Your Angler Dog

Angler dogs' whole lives are about soaking their faces, and so they don't need much training. Simply place the dog on the edge of a river in your favorite wilderness fish-catching location, and light up a cigar. The dog will immediately begin cooling its tongue, the fish will be attracted to the worm-like appendage, and the rest is inevitable. BANG! a strike, and BANG! the mouth snaps shut. When you have half a dozen dogs set out and a school of walleye passes by, life gets very exciting.

Some people think this is the greatest kind of fishing, because unlike with other techniques, you don't have to do anything until the fish is actually caught. Lots of guys just sit around reading and smoking until the dog comes up with a huge fish sticking out of its mouth. A snoozing fisherman might awaken to the pleasant call of his breakfast-cooking buddy: "Flag up!" But before you can pop the fish into the frying pan it has to be extracted from the mouth of the angler dog. With the fish in the caught position, the dog can't open its mouth without help. There is a checklist of procedures to go through. First, nobody is going to think you are a sissy if you wear gloves. Many an angler dog fisherman swears by Kevlar gloves and I certainly recommend them for beginners. If you have a friend that is a pediatrician, a discarded set of forceps might be available. I use the cashew method of extraction. Placing a dip net below the dog/fish union, blow cigar smoke between the eyes of the dog, and cash-shew! the fish is sprung. Works every time. For nonsmokers the cashew reflex can sometimes be stimulated with a feather, or perhaps by putting pollen on the dog's nostrils.

Most of the time I get annoyed at what people name their angler dogs. The names always seem to be evil, violent, or just plain sick. Stan had one he named Squash. I like names that not only reflect these dogs' sweet dispositions but are appropriate to their function. So I started the theme of naming them after my favorite fishing lures.

My all time favorite was little Cleo. She and her sister Phoebe were something else again. Phoebe worked deeper than little Cleo, and she wasn't afraid to get right to the bottom of a bass location. But little Cleo really had action. Some anglers sit passively on the bank soaking their heads. They aren't really fishing, they are simply trying to be cool: any fish they get is by accident. But little Cleo had the best case of wriggle you ever saw. She put a dance on the end of the old tongue which would be sinful to speak about in polite company. Also she would cast about looking for the right spot. You could work her anywhere, and as slow or fast as you wanted. Most anglers just head down the bank to the first place they come to. Not her. She'd collect a little cool in one place and then try to find a hot spot. And it paid off. Little Cleo caught fish.

I often set my anglers first thing in the morning before Stan gets up. That way there is often something else to stick to the pan besides potatoes. In this high cholesterol phase of human evolution, fish can be an important alternative source of protein for the late morning angler. You must bear in mind, though, that fish taken by and from angler dogs have to be prepared differently than fish taken by other forms of fish retrieval. Angler-caught fish are the equivalent of ground round, and your breakfast will be made from the same parts of a fish as a hot dog is from a cow. The good news is, your dressing percentage is higher than if you were doing pure fillets. Angler dog fish are more purée than that. Stan doesn't seem to mind; he manages to blend the fish in with everything else in an unnoticeable way.

TIPPUPS

Tippups may be the most highly evolved animal on earth. In biological terms, that simply means that they are better adapted to their niche than any other living animal. Perhaps they even approach perfection in a dog breed: certainly they are unique among the fishing dogs. Attention has been paid to every single detail of their conformation, a fine tuning that doesn't whistle in the wind. They are so sharp that it's a flat chance the AKC will ever get their number.

Tippups are also the only breed I know that are named after a machine. Usually machines are named after dogs. Bulldogs are the symbol of doggedness, ergo the Mack truck; or fleetness, hence the Greyhound bus. Or ball teams are named after breeds: the Huskies; the Bulldogs; the Consolidated Hairlesses. Youngsters playing softball have the Lassie League.

Tippups are specialists in the ice fishing division of angling sports. Whoever first got the idea that you could use a dog to replace the old-fashioned mechanical "tip-up" is lost to history. If you had to take a wild guess as to which group of sportsmen don't write a lot, naming ice fishermen would keep you in the contest. Ice fishermen are a cold bunch, and often they can't move their fingers for weeks. Similarly, their oral traditions can seldom be deciphered, though with a liberal application of lip camphor you can occasionally get a frosted simile.

Ice Fishing with Tippup Pups

If you have never been ice fishing, you have no idea how cold it s out there in the middle of some godforsaken lake in February. Big frozen lakes have several ecological characteristics that only the expert fully appreciates. Take the words in order:

BIG. This is always an understatement. One rule of ice fishing is that you will find that the lake is much bigger than you thought. Mounting an expedition to the center of the lake is the stuff of National Geographic television specials. Why the center? Remember Stan's rules: if you are on shore, the fish are in the middle of the lake; if you are in the middle of the lake, the fish are on the far side; always cast as far as you can away from you. Well, the same rules apply in the winter, with a little modification—you'd look a little daft standing in the snow in a blizzard casting a frozen minnow out on the ice. You must walk[4]—or drive—to the middle of the lake, and then to the far side. You never see anybody, no matter how naive and inexperienced, cut a hole in the ice beside the parking lot. Absolutely unheard of.

FROZEN. The other first rule of ice fishing is, ice fishing doesn't take place on nice days. Frozen is a word that has to be defined carefully. It would be easier here if I used technical and scientific terms. Lakes are large bodies of water. Lake water is layered, and each layer is a different temperature. The bottom of the lake is the hypolimnon. In the summer the hypolimnon is the coldest layer of the lake, about 39°F. In the winter it is the warmest layer of the lake, still

---

4 If you do anticipate walking, I suggest you consult with Amundsen Apparels, 3333 Itzcold Fiord St., Keerize, N.N. 0001 Norway.

39°F. As you may have already deduced, the layers of a lake turn over from one season to the next; that is because wherever there is 39° water it goes to the bottom. The epilimnon is always on top no matter what the temperature is. But, the epilimnon of summer becomes the warm hypolimnon of winter, even though the bottom remains the same temperature all year 'round.

In the summertime, fish are too hot at the top of the lake and go to the cool bottom (39°). In the winter, the top is too cold for fish, so they prefer the warm bottom (39°). Unless you are a fish, spending too much time in the hypolimnon at any season of the year is bad, so we must move on.

In a frozen lake, the top layers are somewhat anomalous. The lake is not exactly covered with ice. The lake is covered with wind, the hyperzephyrlon. The next layer below the wind layer and above the ice is very interesting: it consists of an unstable mixture of more or less wet shifting slush above the layer of rain water that lies on the ice below.

The hyperzephyrlon always contains water particles in one or more of three forms—snow, sleety wind, or rain. Each form of water sticks to the lake and insulates the adjoining layers from the form of water directly below it. Snow insulates the rain form on top of the ice from the colder wind above. Wind is the gaseous form of water and gets much colder than ice, which has a fixed temperature but is invariably cold.

The form of water particles in the hyperzephyrlon is inversely correlated with temperature: Arctic and Canadian cold fronts bring rain; warm Gulf air causes blizzard snow conditions. On nice days, you fish in between the sleets.

It is complicated and difficult to explain. To put it in simple English (for the German edition, I'm sorry, but there isn't any simple German), each change of precipitation cakes on the ice with a frosting of snow on top, sandwiching the heavier rain water between the sleeting above and icing below. The rain percolates through the snow filter, settling on the ice that is floating on the top of the lake water, which is warmest at the bottom.

And now for a quick lesson on walking to the middle of the lake. Step slowly. Pick a foot up and move it forward a short distance. Compact the snow with the bottom of your boot until you come to the sleet layer. Now shift your weight forward onto the sleet layer (sometimes called a crust because of its brittle and flaky quality). As your weight comes onto the crust you shouldn't have any trouble breaking through. Your foot will quickly settle to the firm ice below the rain water. Wait a second until your boot fills up, then repeat the process with the other foot. Driving to the middle of the lake might be quicker, but walking back to get a tow truck would negate any time saved; the walk, however, does provide adequate exercise to make the experience worthwhile.

When you get to the middle of the lake you must chop a hole in the ice. First, find a place where the ice is thin. This is usually under the pickup truck. Next, a hole must be cleared above the ice. The snow and sleet are easier to clear than the rain water, and fishermen often leave that where it is—chopping a hole underneath this water is not impossible. Hole sizes vary. They should be as deep as the ice is thick. Never make the hole so wide that you could get a fish through it. Wide holes jinx fishing. Besides, wide holes don't refreeze as fast, and you won't have anything to do to keep you moving if the holes aren't refreezing. And finally, too big a hole allows the water on top of the ice to drain too fast into the water under the ice, and that creates little downward whirlpools.

Now chop a minnow out of the bait pail and breathe on him for a few minutes until he becomes lively again. You are simultaneously breathing on your hand, which feels good, but not for long. Lower the lively minnow down through the ice; if the top water is still pouring through the hole, the minnow will be conveniently sucked down. Attach your line to the tip-up. This is a spring-loaded mechanical device consisting of an anti-suck-through-the-ice base, a spool of line, and a spring-loaded flag. When a fish pulls the line, the flag goes from the down position to the up position. Then everybody runs around yelling "FLAG, FLAG!" Some guy halfway down the lake yells, "Flag!" at us. "Stan," I say, "You gotta flag."

Many times during ice fishing you won't get a flag. Often that is because no fish has pulled on the line. Other times it is a combination of factors. For example, the flag gets frozen into the ice because no fish has pulled on it for such a long time.

I know this isn't an ecology book on Nearctic lake dynamics or a "how to" book on ice fishing, but many readers will not appreciate the finer points of tippup dogs if they don't understand the niche these dogs are expected to fill.

Oftentimes (once) during the winter when there is no other act in town Stan'll suggest ice fishing. Off we go with the old-fashioned metal tip-ups and ice augers and all the sweaters in the world.

Believe me, it doesn't ever take me more than thirty seconds to remember how miserable ice fishing can be, especially with Stan. Then we get out of the car. Each fisherman on our lake is allowed twelve tip-ups. That means we get to set up twenty-four between us. That means twenty-five holes (Stan needs an extra for perch jigging). We always start off with good intentions, but Stan can't resist testing the waters, so to speak. I've never said this in print before, but (in my opinion) Stan is a compulsive perch jigger.

A perch jigging rod is normally about a foot long. Stan has a custom-made three-quarter length, four-piece rod. Each piece is cleverly designed to look like a ballpoint pen.

You just *know* that when a guy has a collapsible perch jigging rod hidden in his ice outfit, he's not really focused on the job at hand. I've told the therapist about Stan's jigging rod. You never really see it until out it comes.

And it never comes out until the first hole is chopped. "Let's see if there is anybody down there," he'll say.

"Well, you take a look-see," I'll say cheerfully, trying to be supportive and not to aggravate his condition. All the time I'm thinking, *I'm never, never going ice fishing again. Never.* "I'll set up the twenty-four tip-ups, after I've chopped twenty-four holes in the water, I don't mind." And I sort of don't; it kind of takes my mind off how my feet feel.

Anyway, not so as to make a big deal of the whole thing, I'll drill twenty-four (read twenty-five) holes and carry each of the twenty-four tip-ups to each of twenty-four holes, and set up the twenty-four tip-ups, and hand-warm the twenty-four suckers and reset the flags that have blown loose because the wind is blowing forty-five miles per hour, and if the flag hasn't blown out and over I'll go look at it to see why not, and it's usually because the hole has refrozen because it's 40°F below zero (-40°C).

By this time Stan will have discovered half a five-gallon pail full of four-inch perch right in that very first hole. Can you imagine that? If I could just get the Fish and Game people to change the daily limit from no limit to maybe six yellow perch, I'd be a happy truck owner. That might seem a little obscure (and even a little stingy) to a few of you, but realize that it's really cold out there, so Stanley sits in the passenger seat (more leg room) of my pickup (Stanley doesn't own a pickup), with the engine running (better heat), and cleans the eighty-seven four-inch perch on the open glove compartment door.

Tippup Breed Standard and Training

Tippups were developed in Quebec, and I've come across two different versions of how they came about. One tradition has it that eastern Canadian pike pointer fishermen looking for methods of keeping their dogs exercised in the winter were the first to realize that the dogs could stick their heads down a hole just as well as over the side of a boat. I also heard that the tippups were derived from the angler dogs whose owners who were trying to conserve refrigerator ice and were parking them on lakes in the winter, giving their dogs the best possible face soak. Only an angler dog could enjoy a hole in the ice so much.

But the real story is that tippups were the creation of French Canadians, the finest dog breeders in the world. The rumor is that they ignore all the accepted methods of breed development: if they need a good dog they simply drive around Quebec until they find a volunteer. The truth of the breed's development lies between these traditions. The original tippup was a cross between the angler dog and the pike pointer.

One time up on Lake Champlain I was talking to this Vermonter, and one thing led to another the way it does with a Vermonter. He told me about some tippup dogs he was thinking of buying. I'd never heard of tippups. (Technically that's probably not correct: I had probably heard people talking about them but it didn't make any impression because I don't speak French. Now of course it is all clear to me when I hear, "Le chien du lac, zat iss un teabeauxp auxp, n'est-ce pas?")

It wasn't long after this that I found myself chez Jean Jacques Emile Baptiste (Shorty) St. Codeaux, by a kennel full of tippup pups. Since he was the third son, he was called Emile. (The fifth son was Shorty.) Emile is one of those savoir-dog guys who knows all the ins and outs of tippupping. The afternoons I spent shouting about dogs with him and his ice fishing buddy, Bugle Bill Stapes, were just pure pleasure. B.B. Stapes always talked LOUDLY because evidently Emile doesn't understand English if it is spoken softly.

In the old days of tippups with straight, skinny tails, when a fish struck and the dog tried to go into tip-up position, the frozen-in tail flag would often prevent the proper behavior, leading to torn flags and nasty back injuries. A kettle of hot water was often a necessity for the first tippup-using fishermen.

Emile's highly bred strain has quilted coat patterns that provide maximum protection from strong winds and precipitation in the hyperzephyrlon. Those with checkerboard coloring are nice—much more sought after than the single-colored ones. The only undesirable color is white: on a big lake during a snow squall, small white dogs get run over by skidooers, which seriously limits their usefulness.

Emile explained to me that good tippups shouldn't have a lot of feathering on their legs, because they get frozen in the ice. To counter this, Emile's dogs have the fat tail, very much like the fat-tail sheep so common in desert country. But B.B. Stapes TOLD me that the fat tails of the fishing dogs are functionally different from those of sheep. Fat-tail sheep use their tails for water storage.[5] But fat-tail tippup pups grow the tail to sit on. This built-in insulated cushion keeps certain parts of the dog from getting frozen, or frozen in, as it spends vigilant hours looking into its own ice hole. In turn, the heat of the dog's body keeps ice from forming around the tail and freezing it to the ice.

The other advantage of fat tails, Emile explained, is that in the summer he can leave the dogs for weeks without food or water, when his family and B.B.'s go on vacation. The dog can digest its tail fat for calories, and every time it digests one molecule of fat it gets two molecules of water to go with it, just like the camel. The danger of treating a dog

---

5 When you digest fat you get water; a camel's hump is actually fat, which stores water. So really the way to have enough water on the desert is to eat too much, not drink too much as is commonly thought.

like a camel is that so many dogs are so fat that if people stopped feeding them they would drown from the inside out.

B.B. deescribed to me the advances in tippup pup ear design. A good working tippup doesn't have either pendulous or prick ears. Both are faults, and it should be obvious why. Let's say your tippup pup had ears like a beagle's and spent all day sitting motionless in front of its own ice hole with its nose close to the water, watching intently. The tips of its ears might freeze into the lake: think of discovering that just before dark—now what do you do? You could chip

TIPPUPS

out the ice around the ears, making sure you don't chip an ear, take the twelve dogs home, sit them semi-circularly in front of the fire, and let the twenty-four clumps of ice melt. But all the way home in the pickup truck the twenty-four clumps of ear-based ice would have been swinging back and forth at the ends of the pendulous ears, hurting other dogs, or denting the sides of the truck.

Similarly, the prick-ear-tipped tippup pup's ears would freeze, making the whole ear like a capless pop bottle top moaning in the wind and driving the dog cuckoo. Cuckooed tippup pups with the wind whistling in their frozen ears make eerie, unpleasant sounds, which doesn't add much joy to an otherwise cold and dismal day.

Tippups with big furry ears that bend in the middle (tulip ears) are now the breed standard. The upper half comes down and inward. A special muscle (the *pinna collecta*) draws the inner side of the upper ear against the inside of the lower ear and across the face of the hole leading to the dog's brain. This prevents the dog from getting frozen ear parts. Some people complain that the dog can't hear when the woolly ear is held tightly in the plug position, but as B.B. Stapes SAYS (and he should know), "THEY CAN'T HEAR WITH THEIR ANVILS FROZEN TO THEIR STIRRUPS, EITHER." The fur at the ends of their ears is very long and on really cold days you should tie them together under the tippup's chin for extra warmth.

Tippups have an *epicanthus* in each eye giving them a slightly Mongolian look. These *epicanthi* are Lamarckian in that tippup offspring inherit the perpetual parental squint, preventing snow blindness.

You can't imagine how very excited I got when I discovered these chiens du lac. It wasn't long before I was off to chez moi with a quilted tippup puppy and two plastic ice holes.

It is unbelievably easy to train tippup pups: merely start them young and use plastic ice holes. Use holes as food dishes; then whenever they want to eat they will automatically go to an ice hole. Keep slush in the freezer and cover their food with it. This teaches them to keep the holes clean so they won't miss anything. Feed the dogs at random times. This conditions them to look into the holes constantly.

The artificial ice hole has gone through an evolution of its own. The originals were hand operated and are now something of a collector's item. You occasionally see a reasonably priced one at a tag sale because some widow doesn't know what it is. Early Vermonters used to make them out of leaky bedpans, which was typical of Yankee ingenuity—the bedpans' white color was perfect. The trainer would drop a dog yummy down the pee-wee stem hole at the top, so it would appear suddenly in the larger viewing hole below. Some of my very best ice-hole–attentive dogs were trained on bedpans.

Even though tippups became popular, leaky bedpans never did. There was sort of a supply and demand crisis for bedpans, with yuppy tippup fishermen resorting to buying new. Vermonters started manufacturing them, and it has turned out to be an entrepreneur's dream. First came the basic model, the dedicated ice hole, and then a whole series with patented mechanical extras. The self-winding ice hole randomly presents tidbits, mimicking the random pattern of catching Vermont fish. There was an economy model, but it never worked quite right. Some models put out little puffs of dog food odor, similar to a Pavlovian bell, to keep up the dog's hopes that the ice hole will soon yield a yummy. The electric refrigerated ice hole made its own slush.

Nowadays, of course, there are electronic ice holes designed to use the psychological principles of Skinnerian instrumental conditioning. These present the stimulus at irregular intervals, accompanied by appropriate olfactory reinforcers and the slight hint of punishment if the dog doesn't show the ice hole reflex within the prescribed stimulus period.

Really good ice holes come with ozone-friendly refrigeration attachments. The water ices over and prevents the dog yummy from being retrievable. The dog learns not only to keep the apparatus clear of slush, but also to keep his ears out of his ice hole. The tape deck attachment allows you to play arctic sounds, with authentic howling hyperzephyrlonian wind music that is administered with jet nozzles. For about $999.98, you get a pretty nice ice hole.[6]

A friend who has tippups is a joy during holiday seasons. The number of little accessory gifts that can be purchased is practically endless. Monogrammed pads for the pup to sit on are popular items, as are tippup pup pup tents, which are a cheaper (and lighter) substitute for the tippup ice shacks for individual dogs. A little extra money gets you the dog's whole name on it. Tippup harnesses allow the dog to tow his own ice shack to location, or you could train a team of them to tow everything out there, including you. There is no end to the delights of these dogs.

I gave Stanley a started tippup pup for Christmas one year, thinking he might take some pride in watching the dog work. But, like so many things, it ended in disaster. Stan goes and names the dog Flag. One Sunday afternoon on Lake Winnipesaukee with the fish biting good, the poor dog ran itself silly.

---

6 One severe problem we have at our house is keeping the angler dogs out of the plastic ice holes. Why not buy one for them, you ask? Lookit, if you think I can afford 1000 bucks just to make a tongue-soaking dog happy, you're incorrect. The other severe problem is Stanley. When we have him and his wife over socially, Stan always comes through the door assembling his perch jigging rod, ready to jig the dogs' ice holes.

Epilogue:
The Tail Wags the Dog

ONCE YOU BECOME AN EXPERT ON SOMETHING, YOUR phone rings constantly. As the world's authority on fishing dogs, I get lots of calls. Typically, people ask me if I have any good stock tips or what do I think about some recent political event. Often they use the opportunity to tell me a pretty fishy story about how smart their dog Ralph is.

Many conservation-minded West Coasters don't think of their questions until eleven o'clock at night. This is useful because phone rates are much lower then. Being a morning person, I'm usually cheerful at two a.m.

"Lookit," I say, "I'll see what I've got on conjunctivitis of flounderhounders and call you right back." Sometimes I have to call them right back after a couple of hours to seek clarification. "Is that the left or right eye?" I ask. You see, one eye is in the ancestral position, while the other is in the descendant position, which is moving up. The dog could be suffering from migrating headaches.

Quite often questions are about breeding. Breeding, say, two different breeds of dogs together. Crossbreeding. Crossbreeding fishing dogs.

Crossbreeding is a favorite topic for the wee hours. Not because the phone rates are cheaper, but because this is one of the subjects people don't want to be seen talking about.

All the best fishing dog breeds started with a single individual. Since it was the one that had the original mutation, the one that looked like what all the rest that were to come should look like, it had to be perfect. How on earth could you get anything better than perfect? Why would you want to crossbreed it with anything?

As one night owl put it, "It took seven thousand years to perfect floating mat dogs: who has the right to put asunder what God hath wrought?" It was not exactly a question.

After the original perfection there was a steady line of deterioration. This is true of all creatures but especially true of dogs. We must strive to stay as close as possible to that original perfection. You can't crossbreed to gain perfection, because you wouldn't know which perfection you'd get (if any). Simply put, no breed of dogs is what it used to be; it is practically impossible to get a breed back to its original state even if the line is pure; and if it gets crossed up, by definition it can never be pure again.

There are behavioral problems with crossbreeding too: if you crossbreed, what is the mutt supposed to do? Remember, in order to behave properly dogs are supposed to do what they look like. How can a dog behave nicely if it looks like a crossbreed? For example, what if a tippup crossed with a log dog produces a deadhead? Deadheads are old waterlogs floating just beneath the surface whose job it is to dent boat bottoms and bend propellers. Stanley always keeps a sharp eye out for deadheads and so far we have been able to out-smart them. Knock on wood.

Even though we know that mongrels make the best pets, the best dogs with kids, the best circus performers, and so on *ad infinitum*, that is hardly the point. Breeders are not in the game to make good pets or circus dogs. (And there isn't a great market for circus dogs anyway.) Breeders aren't opposed to making dogs that are good for something, it is just that that is not their job. Their job is to preserve a breed's original purity and bring the breed up to a visual standard. Given the nature of dogs this is very hard, and takes intense concentration. Besides, pure breeders, like pure scientists, would lose face with their peers if they attempted something useful.

A few of my post-midnight callers will protest that con-tinued breeding of pure to pure is really just incestuous inbreeding. In order to stay healthy, don't all breeds need an occasional shot in the genes, some mute-ants in the pants? Of course not! Crossbreeding has to be accidental; out of wedlock, so to speak. If it happens naturally it's kind of okay. But you shouldn't plan it. Besides, each breed should only have one set of genes, the perfect set. If we can get rid of all the variation, then there can be no faults.

As you will remember, I strongly recommended not crossing left-headed flounderhounders with right-headed ones: you could get a dog with one eye on either side, which would be normal. God forbid we should create even by accident a normal dog. There is no money in normal, and it's against club rules. If all dogs were normal there would be no such thing as a breed.

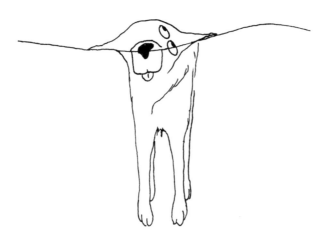

LEFT-HEADED FLOUNDERHOUNDER

Or, breeding opposite-headed dogs might result in a four- or more-eyed dog. That means the dog would always have two eyes in the lawn, whichever side it lay on. And then the two downward eyes would start to migrate up, introspecting the brain. Eventually you'd end up with four eyes on the same side, then eight, then sixteen.

Then there is the question of how to effectuate the copulatory procedure. Would you put the pair back to back, or belly to belly? Don't forget the new back is the right side in a left-headed dog and the reverse for the right-headed dog (could there be a right-headed dog?), meaning that one dog has got her eyes stuck in the lawn again. I personally don't know how people think these things up.

Many wee-hourers persistently have another crossbreeding motive in mind, namely, the all-purpose dog. The result of crossing two breeds, they reason, could be a dog that does both jobs: a kind of two-for-one deal.

A floating mat dog crossed with a stringer spaniel seems to be a natural, until you realize the dog can't walk home. You'd feel pretty dumb carrying a dog home with fish stuck to it. Fat-tailed stringers would be sought after for their beaver-like qualities, and a Maine bow dog crossed with a floating mat might look rather fetchingly like hemp on the bow of a tug boat, even though it would be impossible for the dog to fetch anything.

Personally, I'd never cross an angler dog.

Stanley is always on me to crossbreed our dogs. "Why do we need all these different dogs?" he asks. "One could do everything. Melt them all down into one good Fidue."

"Stan," I say, "You want to breed up a dog that has a quilted Velcro coat; that you could stick seventy-five white perch onto, anywhere, anytime; that has a fat tail so you don't ever have to feed and water it; that floats around the lake casting shade on piscine denizens, which it points out to you with its earthworm-like tongue before it catches the fish itself; and that, just for kicks, has both eyes on the same side of its head?"

"Exactly," says Stanley.